Questions Oneness Pentecostals Don't Ask:

How I See the Elephant

Glen Davidson, M.A.

Dedicated affectionately to my best friend, my wife Nancy.

After all, she has had to listen to me wrestling with ideas for countless hours.

Questions Oneness Pentecostals Don't Ask:
How I See the Elephant

Copyright © 2021
Glen Davidson, M.A.
All Rights Reserved

No portion of this publication may be reproduced, stored in any electronic system, or transmitted in any form or by any means, electronic mechanical, photocopy, recording, or otherwise without written permission from the author. Brief quotations may be used for literary reviews.

All Scripture quotations are from the Authorized King James Version and the Bible unless otherwise noted.

ISBN: 9781718730397

Contents

Preface .... *vii*
Foreword .... *ix*
Introduction .... *xv*

1. The Blind Men and the Elephant 1
2. Three What? 9
3. Let Me Count the Ways 13
4. Don't Confound the Persons 23

5. Let's Look at "Born Again" Again 27
6. Taking Sides 43
7. The Church Split Was Over… 49
8. The "Colossial" Problem 61

9. There's No Two Ways About It 69
10. I'll Take the Fifth 73
11. What Is the Point? 79
12. I Think It's in the Water 83
13. Father Knows Best 87

Summary and Conclusions 121

Addendum I: On the Errors of the Trinity *127*
Addendum II: The Major Creeds of the
　　Postapostolic Church *129*

Preface

This book is written with two sets of readers in mind. If you have not seen the light of the Apostolic message of the mighty God in Christ and the full message of Acts 2, this book is for you. I want you to consider the difference between the days of the Apostles and modern times. First, the generally accepted formula of salvation needs to be corrected. Second, the Christian's view of Christ should be as the God of the universe manifested in human form.

But this is not the only reason for the following pages. If you are with me in the Oneness Pentecostal movement, then allow me to note that we do have our own issues. In our efforts to proclaim the oneness of God, we have been hesitant to examine the distinction of the "persons" (as some would put it) of God. In our efforts to proclaim the deity of Christ, we miss the obvious. He was manifested as the Son of God, yet still maintained his position as the Father.

This study is an effort to be intellectually honest, knowing criticism might come. Only time will tell if I have done a good job. Surely it could have been done better, but my prayer is that God will allow my efforts to be enlightening—for both the Trinitarian and the Oneness Pentecostal camps.

A few years ago, my son David was distraught over a friend's marriage that was at its end. The husband and wife had separated. So my son invited each one to a Denny's restaurant. Neither one knew the other was to show up, but they both did. I cannot say, unfortunately, that their wounds were healed, but at least they were able to meet together and laugh along with my son.

I hope we can meet together. We have been on different paths since 1916 (when the Oneness and Trinitarian movements split; see the chapter 7, "The Church Split was Over"). Maybe we will never agree on everything. But at least let us sit down for a meal together.

Forward

A few words about language:

There is a mystique involved in the art of expressing ourselves. It is the mystery of language. If you have ever stumbled through the fog of learning another language, you will be able to identify with this. Each language has its own syntax, style, and "smell." It is almost impossible to fully translate one thought into another language using word-for-word replacements. This has been a difficulty not only for Bible translators but for every person who attempts to accurately express a complete sentence or thought in another language.

This struggle goes further than moving from one language to another. When we read the words of any author, we must read "between the lines" or get *behind* the words to really understand what the writer is trying to convey. We must not just read the words; we need to think along with the writer.

Some of us have taken great effort to learn the biblical languages. Yet there is still a missing link. Sometimes one word in the original language can have at least two different meanings in the receptor language. The examples are numerous.[1] Other times, two different words from the original language may have one meaning in the receptor language.

In regard to the original-to-receptor language problem, let's take an example: The Jehovah's Witnesses have pointed out that the Greek word for "one" had two meanings: either one in substance or one in purpose. John 10:30 uses the Greek word for purpose. Therefore, they say, Jesus meant he was one in *purpose* with the Father, not one in *substance*. But words are not always the only indication of the meaning. The context of the narrative in John 10 is clear: the religious leaders were ready to kill Jesus—not because he had the same *purpose* as God but because he had the same *substance*; he had "made himself God." This is an example of the necessity of understanding context, not just the original Greek. The problem of breaking the rules is found in any language.

In regard to receptor-from-original language, let's take this example: the Greek words *logos* and *rhema* are both translated as "word." In the late 1970s, much teaching popularized the idea that *logos* meant the written Word of God, while *rhema* meant the spoken or prophetic Word of God. There was even a Bible school named after the latter. While the difference is understandable, the words *logos* and *rhema* are interchanged many times in Scripture. For example, Jesus said that "Man shall not live by bread alone but by every word of God." The Greek word in the account found in one

---

[1] We will be exploring one of these examples, *anothen*, later in this study.

Forward

gospel (Matthew 4:4) is *logos*, but in another gospel (Luke 4:4) the Greek is *rhema*. When we look at the two words in their scriptural context, any modern distinction between the terms seems unnecessary.

The point of all this is that we must understand more than the original language. Yes, we will be examining many words in the Bible. But we must try to perceive the original concept of the Bible writers. We must approach the written Word of God honestly. If we have a preconceived idea, it just may influence our interpretation of the Word.[2] If we are open to the influence of the Spirit of God, as well as the study of the Word of God, God's very concepts will influence our minds and hearts to perceive the true meaning. Nowhere is this illustrated better than the view of God and the Godhead.

A few words about humility:

A constant theme in this book is the need for humility. Our minds are limited. Our God is not. Our understanding is influenced by our own presuppositions and prejudices. Our God can think for himself. To grasp the concepts of eternity, salvation of the soul, and other thoughts that are above us, we are required to do no less than humble ourselves

---

[2] When various translations of the Bible are compared, this becomes obvious. The translators' theological biases invariably play a part in their selection of words. The Italians have an expression: "A translator is a traitor." (The words translator (*traduttore*) and traitor (*traditore*) are very close in Italian, demonstrating this principle even further.)

and let God direct us. If we attempt to comprehend the incomprehensible on our own, we find that pride and error may unknowingly play a part.

It seems that the revelation of God illuminates our searching minds, but it also highlights our own subjective individualism. Understanding that, we should be cautious that our own desire for truth and our drive for standing tall should not keep us from evaluating ourselves: we are carnal beings desperately attempting to find divinity.

This should lead us to evaluate our own opinions honestly. Can we ever say with all certainty, "Our doctrine is pure, and wisdom has died with us" (Job 11:4, 12:2)? Our understanding is limited, though we are seeking after God to shine the light of truth into our minds and hearts.

I do not want to be misunderstood. Yes, certain things *are* revealed to us. The Word of God and the Spirit of the Lord combine to give us understanding. As in the time of Jesus's resurrection, our hearts burn and our minds receive understanding (Luke 24:32, 44). That spirit of revelation should be esteemed and guarded purposefully. This is particularly true when preaching the incarnation of God in Christ. There is power in preaching Jesus that nothing else can replace. In that, we need our boldness.

But boldness can turn into arrogance if we do not also have a place in our lives for humility. After all, what is man that God is mindful of us? It is he that has saved us, and not we ourselves. So let us fight the good fight of faith and preach everything God has given us. At the same time, let us remember: we do not know everything. Admitting that will clear the way so God may continue to lead us.

Forward

A few words about myself:

First and foremost, I am a Christian. I was not brought up that way. I was a secular Jew. We believed in God but did not believe in Jesus. I now do. I totally embrace what he has done for me by the cross. Notice that I believe and preach Christ and him crucified, not just Christianity. I am a child of God by faith in the blood of Jesus Christ.

But I am more than that. I am a Pentecostal. I believe that God moves through the dynamic move of the Holy Spirit. If that does not happen, then my theology of Christ is only a theory. I do believe that speaking in tongues was the initial evidence of the baptism of the Spirit in the book of Acts (chapters 2, 8, 10, and 19), but there was much more. We need enough to carry a burden to this world. We need enough to make a difference. We need enough to say, "I don't have silver or gold, but I sure do have something that will change your life. Give me your hand and let me pray with you." I don't just invite you to my doctrine; I invite you to my experience and to my Jesus.

But I still believe there is more. I believe we must preach the Apostolic doctrine (not just the doctrine of the modern Apostolics[3]). Yes, we are reaching back to the first

---

[3] No critique is meant by this remark, but the principle is intentional. We are not confirmed by our own selves, and never should be, but by the model that was laid out for us by Jesus himself.

century,[4] but God has blessed our "restorationist motif" attempts. The idea of water and Spirit was not only in the book of Acts but was set up earlier in the gospels. The gospels tell us that John baptized with water, but we would be baptized with the Holy Ghost. (See Matthew 3:11, Mark 1:8, Luke 3:16, John 1:33, Acts 1:5, Acts 1:16.) The Apostles had been "set up" for this. They were clearly expecting both water and Spirit to happen in order to enter into the kingdom of God. If only water happened, they sought for the Spirit. If only the Spirit filled them, they commanded the water.

I thought it important to make my soteriology known before we go further. And now, "let us go hence."

---

[4] Years ago I was criticized by a Lutheran pastor. When my son and I told him about the move of God and the Pentecostal experience, he quipped, "I think you are being ahistorical." My reply, instantly given by God, was, "So was Martin Luther." We became good friends. In fact, he invited me to speak about this to his adult Sunday School. Later, the director received the baptism of the Holy Ghost. Finally, he offered us his building free of charge to begin our first (Spanish-speaking) church. Yes, we are reaching back to the book of Acts, and I suppose that could be called ahistorical.

Introduction

It is impossible to write, or even think, without bias. Any history of any war, for example, is colored by the author's personal opinion of causes, countries, and concepts. Nowhere is this more true than in theology. The purpose of my writing is not to naively defend my point of view. However, it would be fair to begin with my own story first.

My upbringing, as stated earlier, was Jewish (both parents, by the way). As is common for about eighty percent of Jews in the United States, we were liberal (sometimes called secular, or Reformed) Jews. We believed in one God, morality, and hard work. We did not want religious foolishness, such as what we thought was Christianity.

My childhood had no special problems. I was known as industrious and a little adventurous intellectually, and it seemed that I would have the capacity to support myself, etc. It was not until my late teenage years that I began, like many teenagers of the 1970s, to experiment with drugs and to ask questions about life. Although my story is not as severe as many, I suffered a great deal of confusion. I seemed to have no direction, and even at that level, the world seemed to be crashing down on me.

My cousin came to visit me one day. He had been a "hippie," along with my brother and many friends. But now he had changed greatly. I was still trying to explore the beliefs and practices of Eastern religions. So when I offered him my brown rice, I made sure I explained its benefits. "This has just the right amount of 'yin' and 'yang'—positive and negative forces," I announced. Mike looked at me with calm, assured eyes and said, "It is not what goes in someone's mouth that defiles him; it is what goes out."

"Uh," I blurted out self-consciously, "who said that?" Of course, he told me the answer. From then, the person of Jesus held my attention. It is amazing how even the historical Christ and his teaching can touch our lives.

Within a short time, I visited my landlord's church and felt the presence of the Lord. To make a long story short, I was baptized. I wonderfully received the baptism of the Holy Ghost a couple of months later. It was after that life-changing experience that my "troubles" began.

A group of "genuine Pentecostals" showed me that baptism had been administered in the name of Jesus in the book of Acts. Apparently when Jesus told his disciples to baptize in the name "of the Father, and of the Son, and of the Holy Ghost" (Mathew 28:19), he was being revelatory, opening up their understanding to his identity (Luke 24:45). According to this theory, when the disciples baptized in the name of Jesus (Acts 2:38, 8:16, 10:48, 19:5, 22:16), they were not contradicting Jesus. They were understanding that the fullness of the Godhead was in Christ bodily. I was rebaptized in the name of Jesus. I saw the revelation of the deity of Christ very clearly. It changed my soul. Nevertheless, I was not sure we had covered all the bases. As a Oneness Pente-

Introduction

costal, there were questions that—well, I really did not even want to ask.

Years later I went to seminary. Two things happened: First, I researched, with the help of a great church historian,[5] the historical development of the Trinity. I became convinced that we Oneness people had more "truth" than we thought we had. We had a historical, not just theological, basis that needed to be declared. Out of these studies, I wrote *The Development of the Trinity; the Evolution of a New Doctrine*, published by Pentecostal Publishing House. I am still convinced of my findings, remaining "oneness" in theology. But a second thing happened: I had a chance to study various ways of looking at the Godhead. Throughout the ages, different views have fought for life within Christianity. My honesty led me to fully hang around views other than my own and attempt to form unbiased conclusions.

Perhaps it could be said this is my Elihu moment. He waited for all the others to speak, not wanting to comment because they had years ahead of him. But he finally spoke up, because his thoughts were "ready to burst like new bottles" (see Job 32:4–22). This year I will have completed living seventy years. Fifty of them have been with the Christian

---

[5] This is referring to Jim Smith, ThD (Harvard). He has taught at Bethel University and the University of San Diego and has contributed many articles to various magazines (and served as an editor for *Christian History*). He was quite familiar with my subject. His doctoral thesis was on the letters of Ignatius, the disciple of the Apostle John. Dr Smith's remarks are on the back cover of this book.

community, and almost all of those years have been with the Oneness Pentecostals. As I said, I am still convinced enough to hang my hat with them. But I do know that there are questions we don't usually ask. In a feeble attempt to do that, I offer these next pages.

The Blind Men and the Elephant
(John Godfrey Saxe, 1872)

It was six men of Hindustan,
 To learning much inclined,
Who went to see the elephant
 (Though all of them were blind),
That each by observation,
 Might satisfy his mind.

The first approached the elephant,
 And happening to fall,
Against his broad and sturdy side,
 At once began to bawl:

Questions Oneness Pentecostals Don't Ask

"God help me! —but the elephant,
 Is truly like a wall!"

The second, feeling of the tusk,
 Cried: "Ho! what have we here,
So very round and smooth and sharp?
 To me 'tis mighty clear,
This wonder of an elephant,
 Is truly like a spear!"

The third approached the animal,
 And happening to take
The squirming trunk within his hands,
 Thus boldly up and spake:
"I see," said he, "the elephant
 Is truly like a snake!"

The fourth reached out his eager hand,
 And felt about the knee.
"What most this wondrous beast is like
 Is mighty plain," said he;
"Tis clear enough the elephant
 Is truly like a tree."

The fifth, who chanced to touch the ear,
 Said, "E'en the blindest man
Can tell what this resembles most;
 Deny the fact who can,
This marvel of an elephant
 Is truly like a fan!"

The Blind Men and the Elephant

The sixth, no sooner had begun
About the beast to grope,
Then seizing on the swinging tail,
That fell within his scope,
"I see, said he, "the elephant
Is truly like a rope!"

And so, these men of Hindustan
Disputed loud and long,
Each in his own opinion
Exceeding stiff and strong,
Though each was partly in the right,
And all were in the wrong!

So, oft in theologic wars,
The disputants, I've seen,
Rail on in utter ignorance
Of what each other mean,
And quarrel about an elephant
Not one of them has seen![6]

When I first heard this poem, it was under unfortunate circumstances. I was at a meeting of preachers of my own faith. Someone from another standpoint had been invited to preach to us. In his introduction, he was honest that he did not see eye to eye with us.

---

[6] This poem, which in the public domain, is usually more antiquated in its language. I have updated it slightly for better readability.

He was Trinitarian, not Oneness. In his message he used this poem of the elephant. He said there were many ways of looking at the Godhead. Then he went on to preach his message (which was not related to the Godhead issue). Because of his introduction, I mentally shut him off, and it was hard to receive his preaching. Now, I do believe that the revelation of the mighty God in Christ is not just another way of viewing the Godhead; it is a revelation from heaven (Matthew 16:17). But I also understand his point.

For those of us who are fighting for our spirit of revelation and truth, it is normal for a poem like this to anger us. After all, what are we to believe? Everything? Is truth only subjective? Our answer must be "No." Truth is totally objective. But we have to also take stock: Just when we think we know everything there is to know about God, we find out that we really see only a part of things. Truth is not contained with us; it is only contained in God, and we receive from him.

I do believe that we need to fight for the truth, but we also need a spirit of humility. There is a huge elephant before us. All the blind men proclaimed what they thought was truth, and yet no one had the whole story. It does not mean the truth was not there. It is just that each understood only from a limited perspective.

Down through the ages of church history, we watch the fights. It does not matter whether it is grace versus law,[7]

---

[7] This is a huge topic. We must understand that the instructions to the church (in the epistles) range from Romans to Jude. Both the love of God and the fear of God are taught. The Bible often seems to pull us one

The Blind Men and the Elephant

which day (if any) should be set aside for God, the will of God versus the will of man (Calvinism and Arminianism), or other issues that concern the Godhead. Each group of blind men, stationed on their side of the theological elephant, loves the Scriptures that prove their view but either ignores or explains away the passages that cannot.

It is enlightening to study the history of the development of Trinitarian thought. What began as an effort to define the difference between God and the Son became a fierce war of identification of words like "substance"[8] and finally "person." Many people take it for granted that the church fathers solved this problem, and so they will just have faith in their decisions about the Godhead: the doctrine of the Trinity, along with the definitions of its terms. It was not that simple. In fact, Jerome, writing to Pope Damasus, complains about how far things had gone:

> I ask them what three hypostases are supposed to mean. They reply three persons subsisting. I rejoin that this is my belief. They are not satisfied with the

---

way with some passages, and then another way with others. Some Bible readers err in only reading one set of passages. But really, we need it all.

[8] The Greek word for "substance" is *ouisious*. The word for "same substance" was *homoouisios*. Then the iota (the letter "i" in the Greek alphabet) was inserted in the middle of the word to describe the connection of God and Jesus: *homo-i-ouisios*. This was to mean almost, or like the same substance. That worked for a short time. Then the arguments began again.

meaning; they demand the term. ... I am counted a heretic. ... I am branded with the stigma of Sabellianism.[9]

The fight continued even long after the famed Council of Nicaea.[10] It would be an error to say there was no more debate. It has continued until the present time. In the 1910s, the rapidly growing Pentecostal movement divided into two camps: Trinitarian Pentecostalism and Oneness Pentecostalism.[11] Each group now speaks only cautiously to the other.[12] This book is not a call for us to "all get along." I don't think that will really happen. Instead, this book is a call for each of us to hear the other out. We must admit that we are both standing in awe, looking at the sides of this enormous, gorgeous, mystical elephant.

You may want to read the poem one more time. I suspect most of us have only one opinion and are not able to live outside it. A mature mind, however, can weigh more

---

[9] Letter 15, Jerome to Damasus. Jerome translated the Vulgate, the Latin version of the Bible, during the time of the "theologic wars" of the Council of Constantinople and the Council of Ephesus.

[10] This is sometimes spelled "Nicea".

[11] Two things may be noted. First, it was not the first division. The Finished Work issue caused similar factions. Second, modern Oneness Pentecostalism may be found as early as 1909.

[12] Recently, there was a seven-year talk at the Society of Pentecostal Studies. That is a good venture. It should be continued, hopefully with even more depth in the future.

The Blind Men and the Elephant

than one answer to a question and can contemplate both affirmations and objections to the answers. Of course opinions may be formed, and truth may be found, but not without hearing all sides.[13]

---

[13] One opinion may have the "anointing," and one may only be natural. (The flesh profits nothing; it is the Spirit that quickens. We should be able to discern the difference with the help of the Spirit.)

Three *What?*

There are "three that bear record in heaven" (1 John 5:7). But three *what*? When William Penn, who was not only one of our nation's founders but a noted Quaker,[14] was asked to find a noun to describe Father, Son, and Holy Spirit, he refused. He said he did not know what to call them; the Bible does not say.

Many others have noted the problem. John Wesley wrote the following:

---

[14] Early Quakers were notably non-Trinitarians. They would be considered modalists (but not Oneness Pentecostals *per se* because they did not stress or believe in the importance of baptism).

I dare not insist upon anyone's using the word Trinity, or Person. I use them myself without any scruple, because I know of none better: But if any man has any scruple concerning them, who shall constrain him to use them; I cannot: Much less would I burn a man alive, and that with moist, green wood, for saying, "Though I believe the Father is God, the Son is God, and the Holy Ghost is God; yet I scruple using the words Trinity and Persons, because I do not find those terms in the Bible." These are the words which merciful John Calvin cites as wrote by Servetus in a letter to himself. I would insist only on the direct words, unexplained, just as they lie in the text: "There are three that bear record in heaven, the Father, the Word, and the Holy Ghost: And these three are one."[15]

Augustine said there was no word to use other than "persons." But that word denotes points of consciousness, separate decisions, etc. In the introduction to his book *On the Trinity*, Augustine was somewhat apologetic for its use. Nevertheless, he used it throughout his writings. The term was

---

[15] John Wesley, "On the Trinity," *A Treasury of Great Preaching*, Sermon 55. (http://wesley.nnu.edu/john-wesley/the-sermons-of-john-wesley-1872-edition/sermon-55-on-the-trinity. Accessed Oct 13, 2020)

Three What?

later used without apology or explanation in the Athanasian Creed, the creed that follows Augustine's philosophies.

So, three *what*? In the modern Oneness movement, many have used "manifestations," but the problem with that term is that in Scripture, the Father remains hidden. The Spirit is manifest, and the Son also, but the Bible never talks about the manifestation of the Father in particular. The word "mode" is a possibility. We may be afraid of the word, since we are reluctant to be called modalists.[16] Nevertheless, it still could work. "Modes of being" is a phrase that Karl Barth used, saying he was reluctant to use the word "persons."

My suggestion is to use the word "personas" rather than "persons." Although no word is perfect, this word will suggest the different masks that God uses for different purposes. The word "personas" also avoids the error of describing God as having three completely different minds, as the word "persons" implies.

---

[16] Modalists, or modalistic monarchians, were supposedly condemned as heretical. Most theologians are aware of this, so a modern movement would not want to purposely be identified with them. Historian Jaroslav Pelikan writes that modalism was formally condemned in gatherings such as the Synod of Braga. But as he notes, this was in the sixth century—three hundred years after the main movement of modalism! Pelikan remarks that "the institution it represented could not be dismissed so easily." [Jaroslav Pelikan, *The Christian Tradition; A History of the Development of Doctrine: volume I: The Emergence of the Catholic Tradition, 100–600.* (Chicago: University of Chicago Press, 1973) 181–82.] There are a couple of differences between the modalists and Oneness Pentecostals, but we will leave that for another time.

Let Me Count the Ways

A Trinitarian friend of mine told me: "The problem that Oneness people have is that they cannot count." Although I was annoyed at the simplicity of his thinking, I also had to admit (later!) there was some humor and logical truth in what he said. Some of us are afraid of the distinctiveness of the Father, Son, and Holy Spirit. We know they are not *persons* with different thinking abilities, but God can act in different roles, offices, or personas.

When we speak of Oneness theology, we are speaking of the one-ness of the three personas. With that in mind, let us ask this question: Would it be possible to speak of the three-ness, two-ness, and one-ness of God and still be biblically correct? How do we see the godhead? How do we examine this elephant? Let me count the ways.

First, we can examine the elephant with a view emphasizing its three-ness. It is the *obvious* way. We cannot deny that the New Testament speaks of the Father, Son, and Holy Spirit. Second, we can look at two-ness. This is the *practical* way—we speak of God as the creator and Jesus Christ the man who was the incarnation of God. Finally, we can look at this huge Being through the paradigm of one-ness. I submit that this is the *revelational* way. We speak of the Mighty God in Christ, not by simple logic, but "in words taught by the Spirit, explaining spiritual realities" (1 Cor 2.13 NIV).

The three-ness of God is obvious on the surface. Of all three ways, it has the least number of scriptures that can be used to support it.[17] Also, none of the passages give the same definitions as the Trinity in its developed stage. Nevertheless, it would be impossible to say that the New Testament does not mention the Father, Son, and Holy Spirit.

Even A. D. Urshan, one of the founders of Oneness Pentecostalism, spoke of God's three-ness.

> I personally cannot refrain from believing that there is a plurality in God's mysterious Being, and

---

[17] Matthew 28:19, 2 Corinthians 13:14, 1 Peter 1:2, and 1 John 5:7. Mt 28.19 is actually a setting of the revelation of the risen Christ. Each of the other passages are dealt with in the chapter 13, "Father Knows Best."

that this plurality is known as a three-ness. Not three separate, distinct Beings or Persons, but a mysterious, inexplicable, incomprehensible three-ness.[18]

Urshan also wrote of the THREE-ONE God (usually with capitals). He marveled at what he called the three *Kenoomas*, a word from his native Persian tongue that was equivalent to the word "personas."[19] However, we need to understand something important. This was early in his journey for God. I don't think there was ever a need for Urshan to refute his early view. Surely it is also true. Even so, Urshan became a legendry influence in the Oneness movement. He went from the obvious to the revelational.

Still, it would be impossible not to note the obvious actuality of viewing the three. But how separate are they? And how do they exist? Have they always lived in communion together? These are thoughts that were developed into the theory of the Trinity as time went on.

Is the Son a separate Being that was somehow alive before his earthly birth? If he was, then we must ask: Was it

---

[18] A.D. Urshan, *The Almighty God in the Lord Jesus Christ* (Los Angeles: The author, 1919) 10.

[19] Andrew D. Urshan, *The Life Story of Andrew Bar David Urshan: An Autobiography of the Author's first forty years* (Stockton, CA: W.A.B.C Press, 1967) 69.

an angel, or a divine creature that was always with God? [20] If it was the *eternal* Son of God who was finally manifested on the earth, does that mean God had not really been alone (Isa 43:10–13, 44:6, 44:8, 44:24, 45:5–7, 45:22, 46:9, Duet 6:4, 32:12, 32:39) in the Old Testament?

The three-ness may be acceptable on the surface of things. In clearly stated Bible terms: God was the one who created all things. Jesus was the incarnation in whom he dwelt. The Holy Spirit always existed but was particularly manifested in power after Jesus's resurrection as the baptism of the Holy Ghost to those who obey him. As mentioned, the combination of all three personas is not frequent [21] in the New Testament. The danger of the three-ness view is it tends to tritheism.

Now let's look at the "two-ness" view. Our term two-ness is new to Christian terminology, but only given to

---

[20] Some of the Trinitarian persuasion have attempted to use Psalm 2:7, Psalm 110:1, and Daniel 7:13 as proof texts for the preexistence of Christ. These scriptures are prophetic visions of Christ that would be to come. Some have also used Proverbs 8:22–23, but this is a clear personification of wisdom, as is done in Proverbs 1:20 and Proverbs 8:1.

[21] We could also explore the baptism of Jesus. I would like to save this for another book or writing but let me briefly explain. God did speak, as he always could. The Spirit was manifest like a dove, but not as a "person." Jesus was fulfilling all righteousness, taking on baptism of water, and the anointing of the Spirit. As the first fruits of the church, ahead of our time, he was in a sense there born of water and of the Spirit. Surely this is a far cry from the "co-equal persons" of that would be eventually taught three centuries later.

compare all three ways of "petting the elephant." There are basically two groups of two-ness people: Jehovah's Witnesses and Unitarians. Neither group claims to be filled with the Spirit. The first group believes in the preexistence of Christ, but the second group does not. An Apostolic organization also used to teach two-ness,[22] but the issue has mostly subsided in their circles.

The two-ness passages speak of the Father and the Son. The constant mention of God the Father and the Lord Jesus Christ in the epistles are too obvious to ignore. We will take about one fourth of this book ("Father Knows Best") to examine those scriptures. But ahead of time, let me point out that in the majority of the passages in the epistles, the writers mention the Father and the Son, but not the Holy Spirit. Little attention was given either in the Bible or church history to the persona of the Holy Spirit until the mid-fourth century. Of course, much attention was given to the outpouring of the Holy Ghost on the first church in the book of Acts. But we are speaking in this book of the Holy Spirit as a separate point of consciousness—as a distinct person. It was not done.[23]

---

[22] The Pentecostal Churches of the Apostolic Faith, which came out of Pentecostal Assemblies of the World. The term two-ness was never used, but the theology was similar. Some have called their theory "adoptionist."

[23] Note that Jesus had specifically taught that the Spirit would not be magnified: "He shall not speak of himself." (John 16:13)

When we deal with the Father and the Son, we begin with the natural realm. But as we move on further into revelation, we see things in a different light. First, Paul acknowledged there was a mystery "of God, even[24] of the Father, and of Christ." Then he said it was in *him*.[25] A few verses later, Paul said the fulness of the Godhead dwells in Christ bodily (Col 2:2–9).

The Father-Son view is understandable in a practical realm. There is one invisible God, and one visible man Christ Jesus. Even so, we must move beyond the veil of superficial understanding. We can examine the results of the two-ness teaching: In the halls of Jehovah's Witnesses, there is very little of the Spirit moving. This is not to be a sharp critic, but it is observable enough to mention. As far as the Unitarians, most (not all) of them merged over fifty years ago with the Universalists. My analysis of this is that if the deity of Christ and Christ crucified are not believed and preached strongly, superficial intellectualism finds a way to invade the hearts and minds of the people.

Now let us look at the one-ness view. First, it is important to fine-tune something. The one-ness of God is one thing. But the deity of Christ is really another issue, although the two are very closely related. We find that magnifying Jesus lifts the soul from sin and despair. Great revivals have

---

[24] See the introduction to chapter 13 "Father Knows Best" regarding the possible uses of "and, even, also" as translations of *kai*. I chose "even" instead of "and" from the KJV in this instance.

[25] The actual word in KJV is "whom" which is singular, indicating Paul meant Christ.

always lifted Jesus up for all to see. But the one-ness of the personas might take a little more thought. Here is a short definition: God can exist as the Creator, become manifest in the flesh as the Son, and be *in* us as the Spirit.

To some, the one-ness view of God smacks of ancient modalism. Tertullian, who came up with the word Trinity (*trinitas* in Latin) threw the modalists under the bus for being too simple. However, their view of God certainly had merit. Millard Erickson, the well-known theologian who authored textbooks for many seminaries, writes:

> Modalistic Monarchianism was a genuinely unique, original and creative conception, and is in some ways a brilliant breakthrough. Both the unity of the Godhead and the deity of all three persons are preserved. [26]

James White, widely known for debates and apologetics, admits that most Christians would be considered, at least in their belief system, as "modalistic."

> I think if we gave a test to the majority of Evangelicals coming out of church this coming Sunday morning on the doctrine of the Trinity, less than half would pass. In fact, I would say we would

---

[26] Millard Erickson, *Christian Theology, second edition* (Grand Rapids, MI: Baker Academic, 1998), 360.

have a 75% failure rate and probably the majority would test as modalistic (Oneness).[27]

Ericson agrees:

In practice, even orthodox Christians have difficulty clinging simultaneously to the several components of the doctrine (of the Trinity).[28]

The view of Christ as God is not new to Christians in the history of the church. Most, if not all, revivals have centered on Jesus Christ. Billy Sunday would often address his crowds simply, with something like "Well, Jesus, look at this fine crowd here tonight."[29] Early modern Oneness Pentecostals noticed that when Christ was preached, the power of God would fall.

The one-ness view of God reflects the earliest documents after the New Testament was written. Jaroslav Pelikan, a noted historian, observed this:

---

[27] "James White Says the Majority of Evangelicals believe in modalism" https://www.youtube.com/watch?v=FPH9Ipfs028&feature=youtu.be

[28] Erickson, 365.

[29] Rachel M. Phillips, *Billy Sunday: Evangelist on the Sawdust Trail* (Uhrichsville, OH: 2001), 11.

Let Me Count the Ways

> All Christians shared the conviction that salvation was the work of no Being less than the Lord of heaven and earth. ... Christians were sure that the Redeemer did not belong to some lower order of divine reality but was *God himself.* The oldest surviving sermon of the Christian Church after the New Testament opened with the words: "Brethren, we ought so to *think of Jesus Christ as of God"* ... The oldest surviving pagan report about the church described Christians as gathering before sunrise and singing a *hymn to Christ as though to God.* The oldest surviving liturgical prayer of the church was a prayer addressed to Christ. *Clearly it was the message of what the church believed and taught that "God" was an appropriate name for Jesus Christ.*[30]

About fifteen years ago, I had the privilege of attending a meeting where David Bernard (who was not yet the general superintendent of the U.P.C.I.) debated a San Diego Baptist pastor. The pastor told him, "You and I don't serve the same God. We can't be serving the same Jesus with such a difference of opinion of who he is." I think we all would expect his rebuttal to be equally harsh. But instead, Bernard, in his kind but revelatory way responded:

---

[30] Jaroslav Pelikan, *The Christian Tradition; A History of the Development of Doctrine: volume I, The Emergence of the Catholic Tradition, 100–600.* (Chicago: University of Chicago Press, 1973) 173. Italics mine.

I do not believe that we worship two different gods. I do believe that he and I worship the same God. We just have different understandings. If I met the president, and I recognized him as the president, and he met the president, yet was dressed casually, and he didn't know who he was, we would still have met the same person, even though we would have slightly different understandings of who that person is.[31]

The congregation stood up and shouted enthusiastically. Bernard, in his humility, stilled their enthusiasm, but the eruption was obviously spiritual. When you are seeing Jesus as the Father incarnate, you are viewing God in the revelational view.

Now, I did mention that I would honestly critique each view. If there were a need in Oneness, it would be to admit: We are very emphatic in exalting Jesus. We should be. But in the definition of each of the personas, we tend to ignore the distinctions.

But how severe is this problem? Let's talk about this in the next chapter.

---

[31] David Bernard vs. Gene Cook debate: https://www.youtube.com/watch?v=G6LXshQf2i0 (0:35:40)

Don't Confound the Persons

The Athanasian Creed was written sometime between AD 450 and AD 525. It was written a good while after the first debates of the councils had taken place at Nicaea (in AD 325) and Constantinople (in AD 381). This creed put a cap—a summary—on the development of the theory of the Trinity. There was now one God, yet three "persons." The Father was different from the Son, the Son was different from the Father, and the Spirit was also a person that was yet different. Yet they were one. ("Try to explain it and you'll lose your mind, but try to deny it, and you'll lose your soul," Millard Erickson tells us at the end of his chapter on the Trinity in *Christian Theology*.) If someone would dare not to believe its tenets, he or she was to be considered separated from the body of Christ. That puts it mildly.

In spite of the obvious danger of falling into the error of tritheism,[32] perhaps there is one point in this major creed that would be agreed with by all of us. The following statement, the fourth point of the Athanasian Creed, would fall into this category. The admonition raises issues that are worthy of our consideration:

> Neither confounding the persons, nor dividing the substance.

This warns us of two possible errors: (1) We could confound, or mix up the functions of the persons, or the personas. The Oneness Pentecostal movement, as well as the ancient movement of modalism, is accused of this error. (2) We could err by overdistinguishing the differences between the substance, thus falling into tritheism.

Let us look at the first error. The warning against "confounding the persons" seemed to me, for a while, to be a valid complaint against modalism or modern Oneness theology. We do need to be aware of this criticism. However, I noticed that in the Word of God, several times the principle of absolute distinctiveness *was* purposely violated. First let us look at the words of Jesus, then Paul, then the gospel writers.

---

[32] Erickson alludes to this also (Erickson, 362).

Don't Confound the Persons

Just before his death, Jesus taught his disciples about the outpouring of the Holy Ghost (John 14–16). He said the Comforter (the third person), would come and stay with us (John 14:16) and even in us (John 14:17). After that Jesus said, "*I* will come to you" (John 14:18). So who is with us and in us? Is it the second person, Christ, or the third person, the Holy Spirit? Or are they the same? I submit Jesus was well aware of the intellectual distinction of the personas, but he ignored it. We could say he purposely "confounded the personas."

Think of some of the other things Jesus said: "If you had known me, you should have known my Father also" (John 8:19). "I and my Father are one" (John 10:30). "Before Abraham was, I am" (John 8:58). "He who has seen me has seen the Father" (John 14:9). Again, it seems as if Jesus purposely confounded the persons, thus bringing attention to the fact that the Son is God!

Consider this statement by John the Baptist: "He comes after me, but he was before me" (John 1:15; see also 1:27). Jesus was born after John the Baptist as a man, but John is telling us that Jesus was also before John! John was confounding the persons to bring attention to Jesus's double role as both man and God.

Paul also "confounds the persons" when he states: "The Spirit of God dwells in you" (Rom 8:9); "Christ is in you" (Rom 8:10); and "The Spirit of him that raised up Jesus from the dead (the Father) dwells in you" (Rom 8:11). So we have the third person, the second person, and the first person living in us! Paul ignores the rules that would be given to the church centuries later through the creeds. In Ephesians

4:6, Paul says that God is above us, in us, and through us. Of course, the same could be said of Christ or the Spirit.

A passage in the gospels tells us of the need to lean on God. Matthew 10:20 states that when we go before authorities, it is the Spirit of the *Father* that will give us the words. Mark 13:11 tells us it is the *Holy Spirit*. Luke 22:1 tells us it is *Jesus* himself. I don't think anyone worries about these differences. My point is that these examples never give us a specific rule to decide which one of the members of the Trinity is with us, in us, or through us.

Now let us examine the second error, dividing the substance. The fifth point of this creed reads: "For there is one Person of the Father, another of the Son, and another of the Holy Spirit." How distinct do we want to make them? The eighth point says: "The Father uncreated, the Son uncreated, the Holy Spirit uncreated." Are these three completely separate and eternal Beings? Augustine, the father of Western theology, developed the doctrine of the Trinity to the next level of the Catholic theology of the three. It was from his writings (*On the Trinity*) that the Athanasian Creed was composed. He admitted that his work was based on the Cappadocians, who advocated separate, coequal, and coeternal "persons."

The Athanasian Creed demands that we "think of the Trinity" to be saved and not lost. From Scripture and personal experience, however, we know that salvation and much blessing comes from keeping our minds on Jesus. There is indeed a mystery trying to understand the Trinity, or the threeness of God. But the revelation of God in Christ is what saves us and keeps us in the realm of the Spirit.

Let's Look At "Born Again" Again

I don't know how many times we have heard the phrase "born again" in our lifetimes. Through the ministry of Billy Graham, current evangelists, and even former President Jimmy Carter, it has almost become a household word. I first became acquainted with this concept in my early days of conversion. I had accepted Christ, so surely I was born again. But when I entered the Oneness Pentecostal movement, my theology was given a seemingly sharp correction: "You are not born again until you are born of water and of the Spirit!"

This term comes from the third chapter of John. The Jewish leader Nicodemus sought an audience with Jesus during the night. He had noticed the miracles Jesus was performing and was apparently curious about what made Jesus tick. Jesus's reply to him was, "Except a man be born again, he cannot see the kingdom of God" (John 3:3).

There is a great use of double meaning here. Before I discuss it, let's look at the term "double meaning." Let's suppose someone says to you, "Call me a taxi." Your response is humorous: "Sure, I'll call you a taxi. Hi, taxi." This joke uses double meaning for the word "call."

One more example. Someone asks you if you will help them fix a car. "So, are you going to help me or not?" Your response is "I am going to work." Does that mean that you will help them to work on the car, or you are going to your place of employment? This is also an example of a double meaning.

Nicodemus noted that Jesus was performing miracles. Really, Nicodemus was aware that Jesus's ability to perform miracles was a sign of the supernatural presence of God (John 3:2). But when Jesus had told him that to see the kingdom of God he should be born again (John 3:3,7) or to be born of the Spirit (John 3:6,8), Nicodemus could not understand. Jesus reproved him: "Art thou a master of Israel, and knowest not of these things?" (John 3:10) It is the Greek word that was translated into English as "again" that commands our attention. In the Greek, it is "a man must be born *anothen*."

So let's look at the usage of *anothen* in the New Testament. We find that the word is used ten times for "from above" (Mt 27:51, Mk 15:38, Lk 1:3, Jn 3:31, Jn 19:11, Jn 19:23, Acts 26:5, James 1:17, James 3:15, James 3:17). We find just one time that *anothen* is used to mean "the second time" (Gal 4:9). But two times it is used with a double meaning: John 3:3 and John 3:7.

Let's Look At "Born Again" Again

Back to our scene. Jesus told Nicodemus you must be born *anothen*. Nicodemus responded, "What do you mean by *anothen*? I have to go back into my mother's womb so I can be born *anothen*?" Jesus responded, yes, you are right. You must be born *anothen*—the second time. You must be born of water and of the Spirit (John 3:5).

So what is Jesus talking about in this situation? Did he mean born *anothen*—from above? Or did he mean born *anothen*—a second time? Let's dig further before we attempt to give an answer.

Born from Above:

The epistles seem to emphasize the concept "born from above," which supports this interpretation. Peter reminded the church that they were "born again" by the incorruptible Word of God (1 Peter 1:23).[33] Peter does not mention water and Spirit here. The use of *anothen* in this verse would be best interpreted as "from above." From the book of Acts, we do know that Peter followed the water–Spirit doctrine not only in Jerusalem (Acts 2) but also in Samaria (Acts 8) and Caesarea (Acts 10). This was his only method. Nevertheless, when he used the term *anothen*, he was referring to the "from above" concept.

---

[33] We find similar Greek words in 1 Peter 1:3 and 1 Peter 2:2. Some of the translations use "born again" and some do not in these other passages. The "born again" in 1 Peter 1:23 is used in most translations.

Likewise, John writes that we can know who is "born of God" by whom they love and what they do (1 John 2:29, 3:9, 5:1, 5:4, 5:18). In his gospel, John wrote that the child of God is born "not of the will of the flesh" but of God (John 1:13). Again, the idea is that we are born "from above." James also writes that God begat us with his word,[34] so we might be new creatures (James 1:18).

Born the Second Time:

We should note, though, that the first church was not established by the epistles but by earlier events described in the Acts of the Apostles. There we clearly find that new believers entered the kingdom of God by water and the Spirit. We see clear examples of this in Jerusalem (Acts 2:38), Samaria (Acts 8:12–17), Caesarea (Acts 10:43–48, 11:15–16), and Ephesus (Acts 19:2–6). In all these places we find the church was born *anothen*—another or a second time.

So What Is It, Then?

What did Jesus mean when he spoke to Nicodemus? Are we to be born from above, or born the second time (of water and the Spirit)? The answer is not either/or. It is both/and.

A couple of things will help us. First, since John wrote the gospel that records Jesus speaking these words

---

[34] The Greek word for "begat" is not the same Greek word *anothen*, but the concept is the same.

Let's Look At "Born Again" Again

(John 3:1–5), what did John think Jesus meant? Second, what did the first readers of John's gospel think Jesus meant?

In Acts 8:14–18, John was sent to Samaria, where the converts had been baptized in the name of the Lord Jesus. Yet none had received the baptism of the Holy Ghost. John, with Peter helping him, proceeded to pray for the Samaritans, and God did fill them. John could not have been satisfied with an experience that was superficial. In fact, he was there when Peter rebuked Simon the sorcerer for his carnality (Acts 8:20–23). John fulfilled the pattern of *anothen*—another time—with these disciples.

What was the early interpretation of John 3:3 and John 3:5? The Gospel of John was written and circulated later than the other Gospels. John's Gospel gave birth to much of the literature written by the post-apostolic fathers. For example, John's use of the word *logos* caused much stir, debate, and defense of the deity of the Lord Jesus Christ. Most importantly, John 3:5 became the foundation of a basic doctrine of the post-apostolic church, confirming baptism. The following is an example:

> They are brought to where there is water and are *born again* in like manner in which we ourselves were *born again*.[35]

---

[35] From Justin Martyr's *First Apology*, c. AD 155.(public domain) Italics mine. Of course "they" is referring to new converts.

As time went on, the terms "born again" (John 3:3) and "water and Spirit" (John 3:5) were used together. At no point in the patristic era can we find a time when the modern born-of-faith-only idea was propagated. "Water" clearly was interpreted to be baptism and the Spirit as the born-from-above experience, although tongues were not necessarily emphasized (as in the book of Acts or the modern Pentecostal movements) as the initial evidence.

Water baptism became even more important in the second century than in the book of Acts. Before someone could be baptized, they would repent, often fast for three days, and finally be baptized publicly. Then they would take communion at the ceremony. At the Council of Constantinople in AD 381, the Nicene Creed was revised to teach "we believe in one baptism for the remission of sins." Yes, this was according to Scripture (Acts 2:38). However, because water baptism was emphasized as the way to enter into the kingdom, a ritualistic, almost legalistic view of baptism began to emerge. Within two centuries, children were baptized, and finally babies. Since babies could not make their own decision to serve God, their godparents were required to speak for them. The Catholic Church currently continues to use John 3:5 to support infant baptism.

The Reformation

Martin Luther took it for granted that infant baptism was authentically demanded by Jesus and the church. He did not challenge this. In fact, he encouraged the persecu-

Let's Look At "Born Again" Again

tion of the Anabaptists, who taught the purposeful baptism of adults. His emphasis was on faith in Christ. The substitution of the Lord Jesus was his theme. His favorite books, Romans and Galatians, were so highly elevated that he found no use for the words of James to show faith by our works. In 1517 Luther posted the famous 95 theses, or points of contention, on the front doors of the Catholic church in Wittenberg, Germany.

Two centuries later, a major reformer openly challenged the definition of what it was to be "born again." His name was George Whitefield (1714–70). Whitefield traveled back and forth between England and the Colonies. His voice could be heard for miles without a microphone. His message was simple: "Ye must be born again!"

What did he mean by that? Whitefield emphasized the message of regeneration and conversion: people must be born from above—the first meaning of *anothen*. He openly challenged what had become the established norm of "baptism for the remission of sins" in the Catholic, Lutheran, and Anglican (Church of England) churches. Here are Whitefield's own words:

> I remember when I first began to speak against baptismal regeneration—in my first sermon, printed when I was about twenty-two years old… the first quarrel many had with me was because I did not say that all people who were baptized were born again. I would as soon believe the doctrine of transubstantiation! Can I believe that a

person who, from the time of his baptism to the time of his death, never fights against the world, the flesh and the devil? No, I could as soon believe that a little wafer in the hands of a priest is the very blood and bones of Jesus Christ.[36]

In another sermon, he preached: "But few of those that are 'born of water' are 'born of the Spirit.'"[37] Here is a fuller text of his message:

> The doctrine of New Birth in Christ Jesus is so seldom considered by Christians, we should be apt to imagine they had "not much as heard" whether there be any such thing as regeneration or not. They believe there is but one God, and one mediator between God and man, even the man Christ Jesus; and that there is no other name given under heaven, whereby they can be saved. But then tell them they must be born again, and they are

---

[36] Online: Retrieved from Joseph Gurney, *Eighteen sermons preached by the late Rev. George Whitefield,* https://quod.lib.umich.edu/cgi/t/text/pageviewer-idx?cc=evans;c=evans;idno=n25065.0001.001;node=N25065.0001.001:17;seq=291;q1=Publishers%20%20catalogues%20--%20Massachusetts;page=root;view=text (accessed 3-12-2021)

[37] Quoted by Arnold Dallimore, *The Life and Times of the Great Evangelist of the Eighteenth Century,* Volume I, (Edinburgh: The Banner Press, 1970), 89.

ready to cry out with Nicodemus, "How can these things be?"

A Christian, baptized into Christ's Church, may be said to be *in Christ*. But few of those that are "born of water" are "born of the Spirit." To be in Christ must certainly mean something more than a bare outward profession. "All are not Israelites that are of Israel." When this is applied to Christianity, he is not a *real* Christian, who is only outwardly; nor is that true baptism, which is only outward in the flesh. But he is a true Christian who is one *inwardly,* whose baptism is that of the *heart*, in the *Spirit,* and not merely in the *water,* whose praise is not of man, but of God.[38]

The comrade of Whitefield was John Wesley (1703–91). When he heard a reading of Martin Luther's introduction to the book of Romans, he felt that his heart was "greatly warmed." He was the pioneer of the Methodist Church, which became the Holiness movement, which was the historical precursor of the modern Pentecostals. So what was Wesley's definition of being born again? Was it just a mental acquiescence? No, it had to be more.

---

[38] The original full sermon by George Whitefield, "The nature and necessity of our New Birth in Christ Jesus, in order to salvation" may be obtained from https://www.gale.com/primary-sources/eighteenth-century-collections-online. Italics Whitefield's.

> Lean no more on the staff of that broken reed, that ye were born again in baptism. How many are the baptized gluttons and drunkards, the baptized liars and common swearers, the baptized railers and evil-speakers, the baptized whoremongers, thieves, extortioners![39]
>
> How is everyone born of the Spirit? ... It is not a bare assent to the proposition, "Jesus is the Christ." ... To say this were to say that the devils were born of God. For they have their faith. ... They, trembling, believe that Jesus is the Christ. This is no more than a dead faith.[40]

Once again, it is important to understand the context of these words and history. After John's gospel was circulated, the church had used the words "born again" to mean "water and Spirit." The Acts model of baptism in water and the baptism of the Spirit was the interpretation of John 3:5 in the early church. But as the centuries progressed, the waters of baptism became a ritual. The birth of the Spirit was assumed to have occurred in the water, even if no experience

---

[39] John Wesley, "The Marks of the New Birth," in *The Sermons of John Wesley: A Collection for the Christian Journey*, ed. by Kenneth J. Collins and Jason E. Vickers (Nashville, TN: Abingdon Press, 2013), 173.

[40] Ibid., 167.

was manifested! By the time of Whitefield and Wesley, the meaning of "born again" was challenged. Most importantly, the term became almost synonymous with conversion or salvation. Almost every (non-Apostolic) preacher since Wesley and Whitefield's time has put emphasis on being "born again" to mean "born from above" and not "born of water and the Spirit."

We can follow the trend through preachers like Dwight L. Moody, Charles Finney, and Billy Sunday. In our present time, preachers such as Billy Graham have used the terminology with almost no question. I do find it interesting that some preachers (David Wilkerson, for example) have decried the lightness of the "born again" experience without repentance.

So, what is it, then? We need to be born again—*from above*—and live a life that depends on the power of God. Salvation comes from heaven. But we must also be born again—the *second time*—of water and the Spirit. This is our entrance into the kingdom of God. We need both—born from above and born of water and of the Spirit.

Born Again and the Early Oneness Movement

When Robert McAlister, from the platform, opened up the Matthew 28:19/Acts 2:38 "New Issue" in 1913, Frank Ewart listened intently. In fact, he took McAlister to his home and looked over all his notes. The next year Ewart publicly baptized his assistant in the name of Jesus, and he

(Glenn Cook) baptized Ewart. From Belvedere, California, the movement exploded.[41]

As the nascent movement moved on, it also developed in doctrine. Some historians like Thomas Fudge[42] have noted the lack of connection between John 3:5 and Acts 2:38 at the beginning. In other words, "born again" was not used by everyone in the movement to mean "born of water and of the Spirit" but "born from above" in one moment of faith. Notice the front article in the first issue (1945) of the UPC magazine the *Pentecostal Herald*:

> Articles on such subjects as "The New Birth" will be accepted, whether they teach that the new birth takes place before baptism in water and Spirit, or that the new birth consists of baptism of water and Spirit. This is indeed the proper attitude toward the most vital subject, as we are all confident that God will lead us into all truth, by his Spirit. It is to be remembered that any and all material written in the spirit of controversy

---

[41] This was not the only event before 1914. The Spanish-speaking revival boasts of the Apostolic movement as early as 1909. Also, McAlister returned to Canada and baptized many ministers between the 1913 and 1914 events. Other revivals have been reported from various countries before 1914. However, this was still an historical watershed event.

[42] Thomas Fudge, *Christianity Without the Cross?* (Parkland, FL: Universal Publishers, 2003)

Let's Look At "Born Again" Again

will by rejected by the Editor and the Board of Publication.[43]

It is quite clear that the use of the word "born again" was still developing in the Oneness movement by 1945. My analysis of this is that most of the preachers that entered into the movement had been very accustomed to think of "born again" as from above. The mark of the Reformers was still on them. It took some time for everyone to accept that "born again" was of water and of the Spirit.

The doctrine of "born again" is now quite strong in the Oneness circles. I do not think we were wrong in our development. However, it would be wise to understand the reason that many have not accepted this definition of the terminology.

The Roman Road?

John 3:3 is often connected to Romans 10:9–10. But can we use Romans as a salvation formula? The book of Acts never mentions that any person enters the kingdom with only the prayer of faith. What about the epistles— the letters to the churches?

We need to divide the Word of God correctly. The Gospels tell of the life of Jesus. The book of Acts lets us know

---

[43] *Pentecostal Herald*, December 1945 (Hazelwood, MO: Pentecostal Publishing House), Oscar Vouga, first article (no title).

what the first church did. The letters were written to the churches that were already *in* the kingdom.

Should we not believe in Jesus Christ as our Lord? Yes, of course we should because we do need him as our Savior. But again, we should note the method of salvation described in the book of Acts. Not one person just repeated a prayer.

Is there an exception to this message in the book of Acts? Yes, we do find that the jailer in Acts 16 was told to "believe on the Lord Jesus Christ, and you will be saved" (Acts 16:31). He did believe, but he also was baptized the same hour of the night! So we cannot use this one verse to establish belief alone as the way to receive salvation. We can see, by implication, that Paul must have instructed his new convert to believe *and* be baptized. We should also assume, based on the other examples in Acts, that Paul instructed him to receive the Holy Ghost.

What do we do with Romans 10:9–10? It tells us if we "confess with thy mouth the Lord Jesus, and shalt believe in thine heart that God hath raised him from the dead, thou shalt be saved." After he had established churches throughout the Roman Empire, Paul instructed the saints in Rome concerning the difference between the Jewish law and faith in Christ. In the middle of this discourse (chapters 9–11) he compares the difference. One way of thinking says salvation comes by what *we* do; the other by what *he* has done. In the second way, the new covenant, salvation is by the grace of God. But this was simply a general review of salvation, not a formula.

What about Galatians 3:26? In this verse, Paul writes that we are all the children of God by faith. But then he adds,

Let's Look At "Born Again" Again

"as many as were baptized into Christ have put on Christ." Paul assumes that his readers had already been baptized. They were saints from the churches of the region of Antioch; now he was instructing them, grounding them in the salvation of grace.

So we can safely conclude that when discussing salvation, Paul may have mentioned accepting the Lord (or having "received Christ," Col. 2.6) as a *concept*. But not once did he use this as the all-complete *event*.[44]

---

[44] We are referring to the time frame of the book of Acts. Paul asked the Ephesians, for example, if they had received the Holy Ghost since they *believed* (Acts 19:2). I am aware that through the history of the church, particularly since the Reformation, accepting the Lord has been the major event for the sinner. Many are spiritually regenerated, though many are not, when the sinner's prayer is repeated. Some are caught in the middle between superficiality and a genuine experience from God. But the point here is not to describe the history of the church after Acts or the Reformation; it is to observe what Paul did in his ministry.

Taking Sides

When I was in high school, the debate club captured my interest. What was asked of us was fascinating. We were to take an issue and study one side of it. We had to give the best arguments for our opinions and then rest the case. The opponents would then take their turn. After this, we had to trade sides! Now this was about as difficult as not knowing east from west. (Have you ever been mixed up when trying to follow directions and had to reverse your thinking until it conformed to the truth?) But the debate club helped us to understand two opposite points of view and still keep our sanity! We were surprised, once we traded sides, that there was another way of looking at things.

Questions Oneness Pentecostals Don't Ask

This study began as an effort to look at more than one view of the Godhead. Admittedly, at the end I still held the "one-ness" perspective, along with some critical observations. However, I would at least like to draw a fair comparison between the two major camps and also give the reasons for my conclusions.

Let us begin with similarities.

Both groups believe in a three-ness of some kind. Each might have a different definition of three-ness, while both camps see the Father as the originator. But the official doctrine of the Trinity is that all three persons are coequal and coeternal. This presents a problem. How can the Father be coequal with the Son? How can God be alone, yet the Son be preexistent with him? Is the Father still the originator of all? It makes much more sense to say that Christ was created in Bethlehem, and therefore we have the Son of God.

Both groups believe in the baptism of the Holy Ghost. The water–Spirit emphasis of the Oneness camp is "over the line" for most Trinitarian Pentecostals.[45] Most Trinitarians believe a person "gets saved"—or enters into the salvation of God—by accepting Christ. Most Oneness Christians believe you must be "born of water and of the Spirit." Until about the 1980s, there were similar views regarding

---

[45] The Church of God in Christ, the largest African-American Trinitarian Pentecostal church, uses John 3:5 in its statement of faith, but in actuality it teaches "saved, sanctified, and filled" rather than water–Spirit as its salvation plan.

the doctrine of the initial sign of speaking in other tongues,[46] but for Trinitarian Pentecostals, emphasis on this doctrine has waned in the last generation.

Both groups believe that Jesus is God. But the "eternal second person" is an issue that muddies the waters for Trinitarians. Was the "eternal Son" manifested in the flesh, or was God?[47] Oneness believers have a problem also. If God was manifest in the flesh (and he was), was God still God? Of course. But our focus on the incarnation tends to blind us to this fact. What a wonder he was on this earth, this man of Galilee. Jesus was fully God, but he was not God fully. God could still speak from heaven. God still remained as the eternal refuge, who begat the Son. I don't know if our minds could ever grasp both truths as the same time; maybe they are not meant to do that.

But what are the differences?

For salvation, Oneness emphasizes the importance of John 3:5 and Acts 2:38. The Trinitarian camp uses the general "evangelical" formula of John 3:3, Acts 16:31, and

---

[46] The initial evidence of the baptism of the Holy Ghost is found in Acts 2:4, 8:17 (implied), 10:46, and 19:6.

[47] In the KJV, 1 Timothy 3:16 reads: "<u>God</u> was manifest in the flesh." The NIV and some others, however, say "who was manifest in the flesh." This could leave the God/Christ choice up to interpretation. However, this is not just a translation issue, but a Greek manuscript difference. I invite you to see Adam Clarke's comments on the passage. His commentary is quite lengthy but worth reading. He attests to the validity of the word *theos* (God) rather than *hos* (who). His commentary may be found on any internet Bible program.

Romans 10:9–10. The early church was set up with repentance, baptism, and the Holy Ghost. John 3:3 is followed by John 3:5. Acts 16:31, as we said, was followed by Acts 16:33. Romans 10 was intended to be a teaching to the church, and its wording was never used as a formula in setting up the church in the book of Acts. The Trinitarian camp uses Romans 10 as an entrance into the kingdom; the Oneness camp does not.

Baptism is strongly emphasized in the Oneness churches. The importance of baptism is sometimes minimized by the Trinitarian camp. Many (not all) Trinitarians will consider baptism to be valid without the same emphasis on its importance. But let us consider the book of Acts and how it describes the context of the baptismal events.

> *Acts 2:* This was the answer of Peter—baptism is for the remission of sins. The word *eis* (for) cannot be looking back to sins that were forgiven. The hearers were looking forward to the future after baptism.

> *Acts 8:* Baptism was the response to the "kingdom of God and the name of the Lord Jesus" after Phillip's preaching and ministry.

> *Acts 8:* After the eunuch convinced Phillip that he believed, he went into the waters of baptism.

Taking Sides

Acts 10: The Holy Spirit fell on the Gentiles. Peter did not leave the situation alone. He "commanded" baptism.

Acts 16: Lydia was baptized, and then Paul stayed there with his workers.

Acts 16: The jailer was told to believe on the Lord Jesus. After that Paul baptized him, along with his household.

Acts 18: Crispus and the Corinthians believed and were baptized.

Acts 19: Paul clearly baptizes the Ephesians in the name of the Lord Jesus.

Acts 22: Paul is told to be baptized, calling on the name of the Lord.

The name of Jesus Christ now comes to the forefront of the discussion. Although both groups highly honor Jesus, Oneness circles give more importance to the name of Jesus. Most obviously, baptism is in the name of Jesus Christ. Among Trinitarians the point of contention is not usually baptism in the name of Jesus but rebaptism. Perhaps the very act of rebaptism seems to desecrate the act of baptism or put too much emphasis on it. I answer this criticism with two reasons:

First, if anyone had been baptized earlier as a baby in any of the other denominations (Catholic, Orthodox, etc.), we do not shake our heads when they are rebaptized in full immersion as an adult believer. Second, the believers in Ephesus in Acts 19 were baptized in the name of the Lord Jesus. They had already been baptized, so this actually was a rebaptism. Apparently Paul did not feel that rebaptism was a desecration.

I realize this is a line in the sand that prevents many souls from being rebaptized in the name of Jesus or keeps preachers from rebaptizing. But when the line of rebaptism in the name of Jesus has not been crossed or when the ministry later pulls back from doing so, it seems like the glory of God—the impact of the honor of God and his presence—is just not the same. I will let God be the final judge in these matters, but that is my observance.

We have covered some basic differences of similarities of both sides. I think we would all agree, though, on one major similarity. We need to contend for the faith that was once delivered to the saints" (Jude 1:3). The general Pentecostal movement once yearned (and hopefully still does) for the church to be fully restored to its first strength. But yes, there are differences. Many look back with sadness at the split that divided the Pentecostal movement into two camps. Let's take a look at that now.

THE CHURCH SPLIT WAS OVER

The year was 1916. The Pentecostal movement had already been split into two camps: the "saved-sanctified-filled" group (Church of God in Christ) and the "finished work" believers (Assembly of God), whose theology was initiated by William Durham. It was later that the question of baptism and its implications rocked or blessed (depending upon your theological preference) the Spirit-filled Christians and preachers.

In 1913 Robert McAlister preached an impromptu sermon at a camp meeting in Arroyo Seco, California. He pointed out that baptism was in the name of Jesus Christ in the early church. He also emphasized the basics of church history, pointing to Tertullian, who notably baptized in a triple immersion style, using Matthew 28:19 as the basis.

The next year, 1914, brought the preaching of the Jesus' name message. Soon connected to that issue was the water–Spirit formula. Within a short time, the Oneness Pentecostal theology spread like wildfire, especially in Canada and Louisiana. G. T. Haywood took the Pentecostal Assemblies of the World into Oneness theology. A. D. Urshan, who had been active with the formation of the Assemblies of God, preached for both sides, but was clearly becoming a spokesman for the Oneness people.

The following year, 1915, was the year of an official debate in the Pentecostal movement. The Assemblies of God had been organized, but the only doctrinal positions enunciated had been Christ and the baptism of the Holy Ghost. It was necessary at the general conference to argue for or against the New Issue[48] of baptism in the name of Jesus. The discussion was tabled until the following year.

The year of the division was 1916. Three years had passed since Robert McAlister and the camp meeting in Arroyo Seco. The need of cementing doctrine was at hand for the Assemblies of God. At this national conference, a statement of faith was written and adopted. The Trinity was ad-

---

[48] The controversy was called the "New Issue."

The Church Split Was Over

opted as "tradition" and "orthodoxy."[49] The sixteen points in the statement included the most important segment: "The Adorable Godhead."

Since this statement of faith sealed the split between Trinitarian Pentecostals and Oneness Pentecostals, I think it is time to revisit the document. Are there points that are good? Are there points to be questioned? So let us examine the first post-Azusa Pentecostal creed: "The Adorable Godhead" of 1916. A word-for-word transcript is given, and my comments will follow each point of the actual statement of faith.

---

[49] These comments are currently used on the Assemblies of God (AG) website. Tradition had previously been despised by the Pentecostals. Howard Goss remarked to E. N. Bell, "I thought we were not going to have a creed!"

Questions Oneness Pentecostals Don't Ask

"The Adorable Godhead"
a. Terms Defined

AG: The terms "Trinity" and "persons" as related to the Godhead, while not found in the Scriptures, are words in harmony with Scripture, whereby we may convey to others our immediate understanding of the doctrine of Christ respecting the Being of God, as distinguished from "gods many and lords many." We therefore may speak with propriety of the Lord our God who is One Lord, as a trinity or as one Being of three persons, and still be absolutely scriptural.

Comments: The first sentence of this section admits that the terms "Trinity" and "persons" are not found in the Bible. But later it states that God is a Trinity. Also, it claims that "one Being of three persons" can be "absolutely scriptural." While I understand that we may use terms outside the Bible, we must be cautious when using extrabiblical terminology.[50] When the decision was made to disallow baptism in the name of Jesus (only), the ministers sang, "Holy, holy holy ... God in three persons, blessed Trinity." The article in the Assembly's periodical[51] described the singing of this "great old hymn." Please note the history of the hymn that they

---

[50] The problematic extrabiblical word is "persons."

[51] *The Weekly Evangel,* October 21, 1916.

| | sang. It was originally named "Nicaea,[52]" commemorating the Nicene Council and the formation of the doctrine of the Trinity. The Nicene Creed, especially in its revised form of AD 381, can hardly be said to be "absolutely scriptural."[53] |

b. Distinction and Relationship in the Godhead

| AG: Christ taught a distinction of Persons in the Godhead, which He expressed in specific terms of relationship as Father, Son, and Holy Spirit, but that this distinction and relationship, as to its mode, is inscrutable and incomprehensible, because unexplained. (sic) | *Comments:* Christ spent many hours teaching, but he never taught a single lesson about the distinction of Persons. When he taught even close to this subject, in John 14 to 16, the personas of God were assumed, but he "confounded the persons" (see chapter 4, "Don't Confound the Persons"). |

---

[52] Written in 1826 by Reginald Heber.

[53] The Nicene creed of AD 325 was revised in AD 381 at Constantinople to proclaim that the Son was begotten of the Father *before all worlds*.

c. Unity of the One Being of Father, Son, and Holy Spirit

AG: Accordingly, therefore, there is that in the Father which constitutes him the Father and not the Son; there is that in the Son which constitutes Him the Son and not the Father; and there is that in the Holy Spirit which constitutes Him the Holy Spirit and not either the Father or the Son. Wherefore the Father is the Begetter, the Son is the Begotten, and the Holy Spirit is the one proceeding from the Father and the Son. Therefore, because these three persons in the Godhead are in a state of unity, there is but one Lord God Almighty and His name one.	*Comments:* This section actually begins by dealing with the distinction of the Father, Son, and Holy Spirit. Then it states that all are in unity. I commend the writers for their attempt at affirming both concepts. However, this follows the Athanasian creed which "divides the substance." The Holy Spirit is never referred to in the letters or other Scriptures as a person.

d. Identity and Cooperation in the Godhead

AG: The Father, the Son and the Holy Spirit are never identical as to Person; nor confused as to relation; nor divided in respect to the Godhead; nor opposed as to cooperation. The Son is in the Father and the Father is in the Son as to relationship. The Son is with the Father and the Father is with the Son, as to fellowship. The Father is not from the Son, but the Son is from the Father, as to authority. The Holy Spirit is from the Father and the Son proceeding, as to nature, relationship, cooperation and authority. Hence, neither Person in the Godhead either exists or works separately or independently of the others.	*Comments:* The premise that the three personas do not work separately would be agreed upon by both camps, as long as the personas are not persons and the Son is not a preexistent point of consciousness before the incarnation.

e. The Title, Lord Jesus Christ

AG: The appellation "Lord Jesus Christ" is a proper name. It is never applied in the New Testament, either to the Father or to the Holy Spirit. It therefore belongs exclusively to the Son of God.	*Comments:* This section emphasizes that the title "Lord Jesus Christ" should never be used of the Father or the Holy Spirit." This is correct. The words were probably written in response to A. D. Urshan's earlier writings that "Lord Jesus Christ" referred to the Father (Lord), Son (Jesus), and the Holy Spirit (Christ). The teaching has not been propagated past his time. The Lord Jesus Christ is "God with us." Both camps should agree with this.

The Church Split Was Over

f. The Lord Jesus Christ, God with Us

AG: The Lord Jesus Christ, as to His divine and eternal nature, is the proper and only Begotten of the Father, but as to His human nature, He is the proper Son of Man. He is therefore acknowledged to be both God and man, who because He is God and man is "Immanuel," God with us.	*Comments:* Yes, Jesus is "God with us." This would fit well in both the Trinitarian and Oneness circles.

g. The Title "Son of God"

AG: Since the name "Immanuel" embraces both God and man in the one Person, our Lord Jesus Christ, it follows that the title Son of God describes His proper deity, and the title Son of Man His proper humanity. Therefore, the title Son of God belongs to the order of eternity, and the title Son of Man to the order of time.	*Comments:* Yes, the title Son of God is biblical. I am wondering if this point was a purposeful attempt to caution members to not use the wrong terminology, God the Son. But how does the title "Son of God" belong to the "order of eternity"? I would argue that "God" belongs to eternity, but the Son of God began in Bethlehem.

h. Transgression of the Doctrine of Christ

AG: Wherefore, it is a transgression of the Doctrine of Christ to say that Jesus Christ derived the title, Son of God, solely from the fact of the incarnation, or because of His relation to the economy of redemption. Therefore, to deny that the Father is a real and eternal Father, and that the Son is a real and eternal Son, is a denial of the distinction and relationship in the Being of God; a denial of the Father, and the Son; and a displacement of the truth that Jesus Christ is come in the flesh.	*Comments:* The title of this point comes from 1 John 2:22.[54] It was said by some that the Oneness camp was blaspheming, or joining the Antichrist, because they denied the Father and the Son. But the answer was that whoever has Christ has both the Father and the Son.[55] The next point needs attention: Jesus was called the "eternal Son." The Bible never gives him the title of the "eternal Son." We cannot find that term used until the late second century.[56] If Jesus was present in the Old Testament as the eternal Son, then there

---

[54] "Who is a liar but he that denieth that Jesus is the Christ? He is antichrist, that denieth the Father and the Son."

[55] "Whosoever denieth the Son, the same hath not the Father; (but) he that acknowledgeth the Son hath the Father also" (1 John 2:23).

[56] Glen Davidson, *The Development of the Trinity* (Hazelwood, MO: Pentecostal Publishing House, 2012), 106. Postbiblical terms with their histories are briefly examined.

The Church Split Was Over

	was more than one that was called God. God emphatically had denied that possibility (Duet 6:4, Duet 32:39, Isaiah 43:10–11, etc.).

i. Exaltation of Jesus Christ as Lord

AG: The Son of God, our Lord Jesus Christ, having by Himself purged our sins, sat down on the right hand of the Majesty on high; angels and principalities and powers having been made subject unto Him. And having been made both Lord and Christ, He sent the Holy Spirit that we, in the name of Jesus, might bow our knees and confess that Jesus Christ is Lord to the glory of God the Father until the end, when the Son shall become subject to the Father that God may be all in all.	*Comments:* This is biblical. This statement should be comfortably accepted by both camps. The question of whether the Father or the Son (or both) is the one who sends the Spirit is an argument that helped split the Catholic and Orthodox churches in AD 1054.[57]

---

[57] This was called the *Filioque* controversy. There were other issues in the 1054 split, but this was a major cause.

j. Equal Honor to the Father and to the Son

AG: Wherefore, since the Father has delivered all judgment unto the Son, it is not only the express duty of all in heaven and on earth to bow the knee, but it is an unspeakable joy in the Holy Spirit to ascribe unto the Son all the attributes of Deity, and to give Him all honor and the glory contained in all the names and titles of the Godhead except those which express relationship (see Distinction and Relationship in the Godhead, Unity of the One Being of Father, Son and Holy Spirit , and Identity and Cooperation in the Godhead) and thus honor the Son even as we honor the Father.	*Comments:* All people should honor the Son, even as they honor the Father. This is the essential point of this section rather than what the title implies. The headquarters of God is in Christ. The Son is exalted. I think most Oneness believers would be happy with the greater part of this section. We absolutely should honor the Son even as the Father is honored.

Summary

Historically "The Adorable Godhead" sealed the rejection of the Oneness preachers. I was surprised to find it lacked a polemic, fighting spirit. I was also surprised to find an admission that the word "Trinity" was not in the Bible. Nevertheless, it its entirety "The Adorable Godhead" helped break the two movements apart.

The Colossial Problem

The letter Paul wrote to the Colossian church has created a colossal (huge) problem! The Jehovah's Witnesses (and the Arians) have used passages from this letter with a theological vengeance to prove the preexistence of Christ and the absolute two-ness, even before Bethlehem. The question to examine is this: What is the meaning of "who, he, his, him" in the main verses of the first two chapters? Let's take a look at these verses.

Col 1:15 "Who[58] ("He" in other versions) is the image of the invisible God, the firstborn of every creature."

Ignatius (following John the Beloved) described Jesus this way in a letter: "the Eternal, the Invisible, who became visible for our sake."[59] What a great way to put this! The Word became flesh, and we beheld his glory (John 1:14). The eternal God became temporal. Jesus, in this verse, is called the "firstborn" that has the inheritance among brethren.

In order to understand "firstborn," we should look at Psalm 89:27. Here God proclaims the child of God to be "my firstborn." Likewise, "firstborn" in Colossians 1:15 should not be taken in the sense that he was born before all ages, as the creeds [60] would later say. Jesus was not born until Bethlehem but was given the firstborn rights among human beings.

Col 1:16 "For by him were all things created"

---

[58] It is necessary to use underlines in some of these next few passages. This is the only way to distinguish between italicized (added) words of text of KJV and emphasized words in the text of this book.

[59] From "The Letter of Ignatius to Polycarp," *The Apostolic Fathers* (Grand Rapids, MI: Baker Academic), 265.

[60] Revised Nicaean Creed of Constantinople, AD 381; Chalcedonian Definition at Chalcedon AD 451

The Colossial Problem

Everything was created by whom? By God or by Christ? It is obvious to the mind that the God of creation made everything. Scripture is in agreement. He breathed everything into existence (Ps 33:6). In this verse, Paul seems to be saying that all things were created *by* him! Does that mean that it was Jesus himself (not the Father) who created all things?

The Jehovah's Witnesses (two-ness preexistence advocates) openly proclaim that God created Jesus, and then Jesus created the world. With Proverbs 8:22–23 and John 17:5 as the foundations for the beliefs, they are convinced that Jesus was made in heaven before his incarnation at Bethlehem and is a separate, created being.[61]

They are not the only ones. In Trinitarian theology, Christ is eternal; he always was. Yet he was the Son. So the eternal Son was manifested. And here, Paul seems to say that all things were made by him, the Son.

However, the Greek word used for "by" is *en,* which is better translated "in." All things were created in (*en*) him, not by him. Some other translations (including the NIV) agree with this: "For in him all things were created."

The letter that Paul wrote to the Ephesians sheds light on the issue of concepts. Paul was in prison when he wrote the letters to the churches in Colossae and Ephesus, both roughly at the same time. Many of the same topics are

---

[61] Their New World Translation says "by means of him (Christ) all things were created."

in both letters, and some topics are even in the same order (redemption, family matters, Tychicus.) There are arguably no two letters that are so similar, both obviously from the same mind and written at approximately the same time.

In Ephesians 3:9, we read that Paul wants everyone to see the mystery that has been hidden in God, "who created all things by Jesus Christ." This is the *same idea* that was presented to the Colossians. We read in the next verses: "To the *intent* that all might be known by the church, which he purposed in Jesus Christ our Lord" (Eph 3:10–11). It is the *intent* of God to wind things up in Jesus Christ. God did not make all things by anyone else than himself. The word "by" (KJV) in Colossians can be clearly understood that it is "to the intent that all things would be in Christ."

> *Col 1:16* "All things were created by him and for him."

We know all things were created by God. But for whom? Can we say it was for God the Father, or for Christ? Who does the word *him* refer to? There seems to be a purposeful ambiguity here. When Paul wrote elsewhere to the Romans that "of him, and through him, and to him are all things" (Rom 11:36), he was speaking clearly of the Father. Yet here, the "him" is beginning to lean toward Christ!

> *Col 1:17* "And he is before all things, and by him all things consist."

The Colossial Problem

All things consist in creation by God. But all things exist in salvation by Christ. All things are also for God, and even for Christ. We cannot separate them. We now detect a switch in the meaning of the words "he" and "him." First, we thought of God the Father, who made all things. Then, we think of Christ, in whom the fullness of the Godhead dwells bodily. The next verse completes the transition.

> *Col 1:18* "And he is the head of the body, the church: who is the beginning, the firstborn from the dead; that in all *things* he might have the preeminence."

Yes, he is the head of the church! In Christ we find the fountainhead of all principalities and powers. Again, we go back to Ephesian 3:10. He might have the preeminence. Who is "he"? God became a man, and God put all "preeminence" in Christ. The position of Lordship was put in the Son!

> *Col 1:19* "For it pleased *the Father* that in him should all fulness dwell."

Note that the word "Father" is not in the original Greek text. The KJV uses italics to signify this. We could say, "It was pleasing" and it would be sufficient for our understanding. In him is all the fullness. This is, of course, in the Son of God. Paul explains it further in the next verse.

> *Col 1:20* And having made peace through the blood of his cross, by him to reconcile all things unto himself.

Now the verse is clearly referring to Christ on the cross, who has risen for us. There is no attempt here to distinguish which persona the "he, him, himself" represents. It is through his cross to redeem us to himself. Christ redeemed us to God. But it could also be said in this way: he brought us back to himself through his own cross. This is the revelational side of the elephant!

> *Col 1:21–22* "he hath reconciled in the body of his flesh through death, to present you holy … in his sight:

Paul repeats his idea to emphasize it: Christ has bought us with his own blood to present us holy in his sight. But is it not in the sight of the Father? I submit it is "both, and."

We could say that God has reconciled us through his Son. But we could also say that God was in Christ reconciling us to himself.[62] In Colossians 1:22, the personas might have been confounded, but it did not matter to Paul in the genre of this letter. The purpose here is to emphasize that God is in Christ, not the distinction between God and Christ.

---

[62] This, of course, is a reference to Paul's comments in 2 Cor 5:19.

The Colossial Problem

Col 2:2 "the acknowledgement of the mystery of God, and of the Father, and of Christ"

What an awesome mystery this is! Only after receiving the revelation of Christ and his cross, experiencing pardon for our sins, do we begin to understand that God the Father was in the Lord Jesus Christ.

Col 2:9 "For in him dwelleth all fulness of the Godhead bodily."

Paul wraps up his words on Christology brilliantly: all is in Christ bodily! All creation is wrapped up in the body of this mysterious man from Galilee. Every eye shall see him. He is "Alpha and Omega, the beginning and the ending" (Rev 1:8). By him all things (of salvation) consist! The very God that said, "I am the first and the last" (Isa 44:6; 48:12) could say it again through this man—and add something new: "I have the keys of hell and of death" (Rev 1:18)!

There's No Two Ways about It

I have pondered much about the use of God the Father and the Lord Jesus Christ. As I was reading one of the modern versions of the Bible in Spanish, I noticed that in a couple of different passages, the translator used a plural verb for the Father and the Lord Jesus Christ! (English-speaking readers might find it hard to understand the difference, but verbs in Spanish and many other languages are singular or plural.) This was a shock to me, because I had always read the singular form of the verbs in the *Reina Valera* 1960 version.

Here is the verse in English: "The Lord Jesus Christ himself, and God the Father, which hath loved us… comfort our hearts, and establish your works" (2 Thessalonians 2:16–17).

The word in question is "comfort." In the Greek text, the word for "comfort" is in the *singular* form.[63] We should not conclude that Paul was attempting to prove that the two are one. He went on with his letter.

There is another Pauline passage with the same issue: "God himself ... and our Lord Jesus *direct* our way unto you" (1 Thessalonians 3:11). The word in question is "direct." Again, the Greek form is singular, not plural.[64]

Finally, we leave Paul and turn to the book of Revelation, where we are told of the end of all things. "The Lord God Almighty and the Lamb are the temple" (Rev 21:22). Both the invisible God and the ontologically distinct Lamb are present. At first glance, we could say that this verse would support two-ness. And in a verse soon after that (Rev 22:1), John records that the water of life flows from "the throne of God and of the Lamb." Then a few verses later, the "throne of God and of the Lamb" shall be in heaven (Rev 22:3).

But this verse (Rev 22:3) finishes with "his servants shall see *him*"—not "them." The next verse (Rev 22:4) continues: "And they shall see *his* face; and *his* name shall be in their foreheads." Not "their faces" or "their names." I submit that while there may be an ontological distinction between

---

[63] In Greek, the language follows the subject-verb rules. Many other languages do the same. English, however, often uses the same forms for both plural and singular verbs.

[64] The subjunctive case in English would use the same word for plural or singular. The Greek, however, does show a difference between the singular and plural usages.

There's No Two Ways about It

God and the Lamb, there is only one God whose face and name we shall see! The elephant in all its wonders has some secret things that only he understands (Romans 16:25).

There's no two ways about it!

I'll Take the Fifth

Yes, I will take the fifth: the fifth verse of John 17. Actually, this is another "colossal problem" for many of us. Jesus said he was there in the beginning with the Father. So, what do we do with *that* if we don't believe he was eternal? Let's look into all the verses of John 17:1–5.

> *John 17:1* These words spake Jesus, and lifted up his eyes to heaven, and said, Father, the hour is come; glorify thy Son, that thy Son also may glorify thee:

Jesus is now praying as the Son. The part of the elephant to pet is not the part that says, "God is in Christ, and he is all in all." No, this is a different view. He is specifically praying as the Son, as the Lamb to be slain before the Father. This had been preordained from the foundation of the world, and now the work is in progress.

> *John 17:2* As thou hast given him power over all flesh, that he should give eternal life to as many as thou hast given him.

Because he has overcome, we shall overcome (John 16:33). He gives eternal life. Of course God gives eternal life, but since Jesus thought it not robbery to be equal with God, we can say that he gives it and be correct.

> *John 17:3* And this is life eternal, that they might know thee the only true God, and Jesus Christ, whom thou hast sent.

He knows one thing is of the utmost importance: to know God—the invisible God that created the heavens and the earth. And now there is an *added feature*: to know the visible image of the invisible God. God is the fountain of life. Now in Jesus Christ, we receive a well of water springing up into everlasting life. Why? So that we might know God. And even that we might know Jesus Christ. He refers to himself in

I'll Take the Fifth

the grammatical third person, which is very similar to what he did with John 3:16.[65]

The Greek word *kai*, in this context, would be best translated "and even." (It is not really "and," which indicates a full separation of persons; it is not really "even," which would indicate a full unity without an ontological difference.) The God of the ages will be known, and now the additional role of the man that went through Calvary can be known!

> *John 17:4* I have glorified thee on the earth: I have finished the work which thou gavest me to do.

Now as the man, he rejoices that his work is done. This could even be viewed as a reference to the sacrifice on Calvary, as if it had already been done. That would coincide with the tenor of the next verse. He is about to accomplish this after his prayer. What joy he must have felt to realize that all eternity and the temporary condition of his life met together at this point. This had been planned by God the

---

[65] "God so loved the world, that he gave his only begotten Son" were the words of Jesus. The "third person" way of speaking would be similar to a mother speaking to her child: "You must do this because Mother said so." She did not use her first name but highlighted her office. Jesus is highlighting the office of the Father, and of course he is the Son. He loved the world before its foundation as God, yet he was referring to himself as the Son. He did not say "I have so loved the world," speaking as the Father. Though God was in Christ, he refers to God the Creator.

Father before all ages, and now Jesus is about to accomplish the plan. These words were spoken as the Son of Man. These last words would be the greatest for any of us before we die. This part of the scene is easy to digest. But it is the next verse that causes us to wonder.

> *John 17:5* And now, O Father, glorify thou me with thine own self with the glory which I had with thee before the world was.

Now this preplanning and the future event (in a few moments) of Calvary are about to merge. He is looking to God, and he is the man. He says, "Glorify me with your own self." The very God of the ages is to be glorified in the incarnation, crucifixion, and resurrection.

But he continues: "with the glory which I had with thee before the world was." He knows that this was planned from the foundation of the world. The glory of the resurrection was already in the mind of God. Still, Jesus was born in Bethlehem. The temporal part of his life was now ending. He was not a preexistent person, spirit being, or second preexistent point of consciousness. The glory was *preplanned*, and now he was about to see it happen. He was suffering as the Son, but as he was suffering (and was about to suffer more) he was sustained by the joy set before him. He was enduring the cross—the affliction, the misunderstanding, and the pain—but it all had been predestined. It was the glory that was with God "before the world was."

I'll Take the Fifth

Some who want to make a scriptural case for the preexistence of Christ have used this passage as a proof text. There are two possible meanings of this passage:

1. Jesus had the glory before the foundation of the world. That would support his preexistence as the second eternal person. The Jehovah's Witnesses, using this verse, adamantly proclaim this position. Although most Christians reject their view of Christ as "a god,"[66] we need to take heed: the preexistence of Christ as a second person (originally an Arian doctrine) was cleverly adjusted to be "eternal generation" (the Son was eternal, but continually generated). It became part of the definition of the Trinity. I submit, therefore, that the logical conclusion of the preexistence of Christ is modern Trinitarianism.
2. The glory was preplanned, and soon after this prayer the events played out that showed this glory.

The second option, of course, is what I support. There are several reasons for this:

1. Peter very clearly expresses that Jesus was foreknown before the foundation of the world, *but he was manifested* in the last days (1 Peter 1:20).

---

[66] John 1:1, New World Translation of the Jehovah's Witnesses.

2. John writes that Jesus is the lamb that was slain from the foundation of the world (Rev. 13:8), yet it happened at a specific time.
3. Jesus told his disciples in John 17:22 that he *had* given them his glory. Now, this was a prophetic remark. His disciples would not actually receive this glory until after the crucifixion and the outpouring of the Spirit at Pentecost.
4. Jesus had previously spoken in similar fashion in the well-known words of John 3:16. God "gave" the Son, which in its context speaks of Calvary and the Son being lifted up. But God had really not given the Son yet; it had still not happened.
5. Scripture is replete with promises that appear to be described as though they were already present but are not yet (Romans 4:17). For example, God promised Abram that he had given the land to him and his seed (Gen 15:18), although the actuality of it had not played out yet.

In summary, it is clear that there has always been one God. An additional eternal, coequal partner in the Old Testament would destroy the basic premise of monotheism. This would make the Old Testament God a liar. God had the glory preplanned and given to Jesus from the foundation of the world. Finally, in the last days after his resurrection the promise would come to pass.

What Is the Point?

The question at hand concerns the points of consciousness. If God is in three "persons," or modes of being, or offices, what can we say about the thinking abilities of each one? A well-known evangelist[67] proclaimed a few years ago that he could discern the voices of each. He said he knows whether he hears the Father, or Christ, or the Holy Spirit. His "revelation" was not well received in the Christian community.

---

[67] I have not wanted to name him, but it is public knowledge that Benny Hinn openly stated this.

The first piece in this puzzle should be easily established: the Holy Spirit never was a separate point of consciousness in the Old Testament. God was never separated from his Spirit. In the New Testament, we find that when Ananias lied to the Holy Ghost, it was the same as lying to God (Acts 5:3–4). The greetings in the letters do not mention the Spirit. The Holy Spirit magnifies Christ, but he does not speak of himself (John 16:13). In the New Testament the Spirit does not receive the emphasis needed to be called a point of consciousness. The debates about the Godhead in the second and third centuries (Justin Martyr, Tertullian) focused on the differences between the Father and the Son, but the discussion of the person—or the point of consciousness—of the Holy Spirit did not come into the question until the middle of the fourth century with Cappadocian Fathers after the Council of Nicaea.

But what about the other two personas? We understand that the Father of all, the Creator of the universe, was God the Father. Then we understand that Jesus lived. Does that mean that there were two points of consciousness?

It is obvious that the Old Testament talks of only one God. There is not another. Is there a God besides him? He knows of none (Isa 44:8). But once the man Jesus was here, we have to consider a major issue. We understand that he, as a man, prayed to God. So while Jesus was here, can it be said that there was a separate point of consciousness?

When Jesus prayed to God at Gethsemane (Matthew 26), he wrestled with surrendering to the will of God.

What Is the Point?

He submitted himself to him who was able to deliver him. But it was more than his flesh wrestling against his spirit—all within one person. Jesus was actually wrestling with God. An angel came and helped him (Luke 22:43). God was well pleased. *In that situation*, we do have two wills, or two points of consciousness. Note again, however, that we are now examining the humanity of Christ, not the deity of Christ. He chose, though being equal in power with God, to cast his authority aside to fulfill the role of the Lamb of God. But he still had a will that was separate from the will of God.

But what about later? After his resurrection, could there possibly be two points of consciousness? Let's consider something—the voice of God. There is one voice that speaks. The voice of God spoke in the cool of the day (Genesis 3:8). But Jesus said we would hear *his* voice (John 10:17). Paul heard a voice from heaven, and the voice was that of Jesus (Acts 9:6). Jesus himself said if we would hear his voice, he would "have dinner with us as friends" (Rev 3:20, NLT).

Notice this important point. The voice of God spoke all through the Old Testament. But after the resurrection, we never hear of one time that the Father spoke. Jesus spoke to Paul. Jesus spoke to the seven churches. Never was there a separate point of consciousness after this resurrection that spoke.

Here is my conclusion. The headquarters of God is now in the Lord Jesus Christ. He does the speaking. There is one God, manifest in the flesh. We can identify two points of consciousness only during the *earthly* life of Christ. Those days are over. He is now in the midst of the throne. All power is given unto him in heaven and in earth. If you want to commune with God, he is in his Son. This is the true God, and eternal life (1 John 5:20).

I Think It's in the Water

Jesus has revealed his identity. The God of the universe shined his light through Jesus. He was the Son of God. However, he was also God himself. In Mark 2 he forgave sins. In John 8 he said, "Before Abraham was, I am." In John 10 he said, "I and my Father are one," provoking the Jews to try to stone him. In John 18 he said, "I am he," as the power of God knocked his accusers to the ground.

But at no time was this clearer than after Jesus rose from the dead. He took food, as he had done before, and their eyes were opened. A little while later he appeared to them. They could barely believe it. Their hearts had burned. Now they saw him. So Jesus did what our hearts are still longing for: he revealed his true identity to them.

It is in that setting that we find the conclusions of the gospels: Luke writes that Jesus "opened their understanding." He told them that repentance and remission of sins would begin shortly in Jerusalem. Indeed, it was at Jerusalem that the new covenant began with remission of sins (Acts 2:38) and the Holy Ghost was sent from heaven.

Matthew writes about the same risen Savior. His gospel has a parallel account of the great commission in Luke. But here Jesus says, "All power is given unto *me* in heaven and in earth" (Mt 28:18). He continues (paraphrasing): "Go *therefore* ... baptize and teach. Get them to understand. I am opening up your eyes. Therefore, because all power has been given unto me, baptize them in the *name* of the Father, and of the Son, and of the Holy Ghost." If we compare Luke 24:47 with Matthew 28:19 and then proceed to Acts 2:38, 8:16, 10:48, 19:5, and 22:16, we can see the whole picture. They baptized in the name of Jesus for a good reason. They were fulfilling the commandment of Jesus and the revelation of his deity.

For almost 100 years after Acts, we find that baptism continued in the name of Jesus.[68] Later, Justin Martyr refers

---

[68] The first time we have a possible change is in the *Didache*. It should be noted that there is much argument over its dating—perhaps in late first century or sometime in the second. More importantly, it is "suspect of interpolation." (Regarding both matters, see Everett Ferguson, *Baptism in the Early Church: History Theology, and Liturgy in the First Five Centuries.* Grand Rapids, MI: Eerdmans, 2009, 201.) However, the baptismal formula still included the "name of the Lord" in the *Didache*. According to Otto Heick, the first mention of baptism changing from the name of Jesus to any three-fold formula was AD 130 (Otto Heick, *A History of Christian Thought,* Volume 1, Philadelphia: Fortress Press, 1965, 87).

to baptism "in the name of God, the Father and Lord of the universe, and of our Savior Jesus Christ, and of the Holy Spirit" in about AD 180.[69] This should show us that the words of Matthew 28:19 were *not yet* being used exactly in baptisms.[70]

The words of Matthew 28:19 were used as a proof text of the Trinity about AD 200 by Tertullian. Please note that he suggested that new souls should be baptized three times: once for the Father, once for the Son, and then once for Holy Spirit. If the words of Matthew 28:19 were being used in baptisms before that time, this would not have been a new idea. Although Tertullian was confessedly a subordinationist,[71] his ideas influenced theological thought. It would not be until the next century that the *Gloria Patri* would proclaim that the glory should be to the Father, and to the Son, and to the Holy Ghost (rather than "*to* the Father *through* the Son *in* the Holy Ghost"). But the seed had been planted.

---

[69] Justin Martyr's formula is in his *First Apology*. Although this may be found easily on the internet, a printed form may be found in *Early Church Fathers*, edited by Cyril Richardson (New York: Touchstone, 1996) 282.

[70] The point of this remark is that baptism did not yet use the exact words of Matthew 28:19 during the second century. It was not until AD 200 (see the next paragraph) that the passage was used verbatim.

[71] Tertullian specifically wrote against the theology that the Son was co-equal or coeternal with the Father (*Against Hermogenes*, Ch 7, 9.15.40, quoted in Davidson, *The Development of the Trinity*, 52). This was one of the reasons why the Catholic Church did not consider him to be a "doctor" of the Church.

Augustine, who later wrote *On the Trinity*, used Matthew's words as a proof text of the Trinity, just as Tertullian had done.

Since some have recently brought up the possibility of interpolation, let us cover that quickly. Since baptism was in the name of Jesus but Matthew records Jesus commanding baptism in the name of the Father and of the Son and of the Holy Ghost,[72] is it possible that words were added? Some have pointed to Eusebius. This first church historian does mention that Jesus told his disciples to teach and baptize "in his name." But it does not appear that he is *quoting* Matthew. Instead, he is *referring* to Matthew's words. Eusebius refers to other passages in this manner on several occasions.

This leaves only one other option. Jesus is being *parabolic* here. He is revealing that the Almighty God is in the Son, and his name is Jesus. The genre of this passage is the revelation of Christ, matching Luke 24:47 perfectly. It was God who was in Christ, who had risen from the grave for us.

The apostles saw the risen Christ. They heard him and digested his words. Powers and principalities would now be subject unto him. Further, he would be with them unto the end of the world. They were to go forth, preaching in his name. In fact, whatever we do in word or in deed should be done in the name of Jesus, giving thanks to God by him (Col 3:17). Should we not, then, baptize in his name?

Yes, I think it's in the water.

---

[72] Notice that it was not "in the name of the Father, Son, and Holy Ghost," as many are doing today. It was much clearer: "in the name *of the* Father, and *of the* Son, and *of the* Holy Ghost."

FATHER KNOWS BEST

Several times this book has said that the one-ness view of God—in particular the deity of Christ—is revelatory. But what do we do with all the passages that refer to God as the Father, especially ones that refer to a combination of God the Father and the Lord Jesus Christ? Since they are in the letters to the church, they surely do apply to us. In our zeal to promote the one-ness of God, we tend to ignore them.

Paul's letters

Most of the Pauline introductory passages are not in a didactic genre. In those cases, they are simply meant to greet the church and not give revelation. That will help us to understand what Paul was saying.

In all due respect to my elders and brethren in the ministry, one issue should be addressed, even it if it is painful for us. It concerns the Greek word *kai*. Some have said that this word should always be translated "even." However, a word in any language has a semantic range. It is not correct for a translation to use only one of the meanings. According to William Mounce, the word *kai* appears in the New Testament 9018 times. In the noted Greek scholar's opinion, it may be translated as "and, even, also, namely."[73] Other times it can be a combination, such as "and even." Each choice depends upon context.

Once again, most of the questions that Oneness Pentecostals don't ask involve the letters. It would be best for us to take on the issues directly. So now our task lies before us. Let us examine each of the passages that talk of God the Father in the epistles.

> *Romans 1:7* To all that be in Rome, beloved of God, called to be saints: Grace to you and peace from God our Father, and the Lord Jesus Christ.

The reader is greeted with the salutation of grace and peace. There are two founts from which they come.

---

[73] William D. Mounce, *Basics of Biblical Greek Grammar,* third ed. (Grand Rapids, MI: Zondervan, 2009), 17

Father Knows Best

One is the Creator of the universe, and the other is the man that was crucified, who was God manifested in the flesh—the visible image of the invisible God. Both have a part in bringing us grace and peace. We trust in God as the Creator; we trust in the Redeemer that took our place. We trust in God, *kai*—and even—trust in Christ. The conjunction links together the founts.

> *Romans 15:6* That ye may with one mind, and one mouth glorify God, even the Father of our Lord Jesus Christ.

Here Paul is highlighting the Father. The apostle's emphasis on the Father is not apart from the Son. Jesus did not come of his own; he came from above. It is the Father that gives credence to the Son and his work on the cross.

> *1 Corinthians 1:3* Grace be unto you, and peace, from God our Father, and from the Lord Jesus Christ.

Since Paul does not continue after this passage with the theme of two distinct persons, this scripture would be similar to Romans 1:7. The *kai* puts the link between the grace and peace of God the Father and the crucified Savior. Paul is not attempting to portray the two personas as one. That is not his focus. Instead, he is greeting the church and laying a foundation for what is to come in this letter.

1 Corinthians 8:6 But to us there is but one God, the Father, of whom are all things, and we in him; and one Lord Jesus Christ, by whom are all things, and we by him.

In this part of the letter, Paul was addressing idolatry. He was not describing the Godhead or how personas related within it. He was juxtaposing the worship of idols and the worship of God. Instead of worshiping idols, the saints should worship God. There is only one God. Also, we have the Lord Christ, who was God in the form of man. As was said before, there are two groups[74] that use this passage as biblical proof that there are two persons. But that is not the intention of the passage; the intention is to warn against idolatry.

1 Corinthians 15:24 Then cometh the end, when he shall have delivered up the kingdom to God, even the Father…

The best way to treat this passage is to look at it in the context of Paul's thoughts. Here it is again, with the subsequent passages.

1 Corinthians 15:24–28 Then cometh the end, when he shall have delivered up the kingdom

---

[74] Jehovah's Witnesses and Unitarians

to God, even the Father; when he shall have put down all rule and all authority and power. For he must reign, till he hath put all enemies under his feet. The last enemy that shall be destroyed is death. For he hath put all things under his feet. But when he saith all things are put under him, it is manifest that he is excepted, which did put all things under him. And when all things shall be subdued unto him, then shall the Son also himself be subject unto him that put all things under him, that God may be all in all.

Our attention is on "God, even the Father." We note the special emphasis given to the Father, putting the highlight on the Father as separate from Christ. There should be no problem with that.

There are a couple of different opinions regarding the continuation of the Sonship after judgment, even among Oneness Pentecostals. This scripture, by itself, seems to indicate that in the future the need of redemption by Christ will be absolved so God may be all in all.[75]

---

[75] A different writer on this subject does present a different view. The apostle John, in Revelation 22:3, shares his vision of "the throne of God and of the Lamb." (Note that the next verse, Rev 22:4, says *his* face and *his* name shall be in their foreheads.) So it would appear that, according to John's revelation, the fullness of the godhead will still be Christ bodily. But we need to take each passage in its context. For many of us, the phrase "that God may be all in all" indicates the function of the Son of God in the future is a mystery.

2 Corinthians 1:2 Grace be to you and peace from
God our Father, and from the Lord Jesus Christ.

This is how Paul begins his second[76] letter to the Corinthians. Please refer to the earlier notes about the salutations in Romans 1:7 and 1 Corinthians 1:3. The idea is the same here. It would not be right to say that the "and" should be "even" in this verse. If we look at the next verse, we see a continuation of thought regarding God the Father.

2 Corinthians 1:3 Blessed be God, even the Father
of our Lord Jesus Christ, the Father of mercies,
and the God of all comfort.

Paul is obviously highlighting God the Father. It is God who gives all comfort. This is not to say the Son is not capable of giving comfort, but Paul makes no effort to compare the two personas in this verse.

2 Corinthians 11:31 The God and Father of our
Lord Jesus Christ, which is blessed for evermore,
knoweth that I lie not.

This is another passage that clearly emphasizes God as the Father. He knows all things.

---

[76] Some scholars feel that it is his third or fourth letter.

> *2 Corinthians 13:14* The grace of the Lord Jesus Christ, and the love of God, and the communion of the Holy Ghost, be with you all. Amen

This passage, which tends to emphasize the threeness of God, is the only one of its kind in the Pauline epistles. Paul never attempted to explain all three roles, offices, personas, or persons. Note that this verse is not written for a didactic purpose; that is, it is not written to teach us. It is the benediction (the ending) of the letter. While it is interesting that Paul notes all three personas, he does not deal with each one formally or definitively. Grace, love, and communion are all similar. The fatherhood of God is not mentioned, nor the redemption of Christ.

Paul did not end any other epistles in a three-fold manner. In fact, he closed eight of his letters by simply writing, "The grace of the Lord Jesus be with you."

> *Galatians 1:1* Paul, an apostle, (not of men, neither by man, but by Jesus Christ, and God the Father, who raised him from the dead;)

Paul's authority came from Jesus Christ *kai* God the Father. The apostle was not attempting to teach that the two personas are in some way the same. Instead, he was establishing his authority. Thus, it would not be fair to say that the *kai* was mistranslated and should have been "even"; surely Jesus Christ is not "even" the Father. Paul goes on to identify God the Father as having raised Christ from the dead.

Questions Oneness Pentecostals Don't Ask

Galatians 1:3 Grace be to you and peace from
God the Father, and *from* our Lord Jesus Christ.

This verse has the same intention as the other salutations. Paul is not trying to prove that there are two persons by using *kai*, nor does he want us to point out the one-ness of personas by using this word. In greeting the church, he is emphasizing the grace and peace that come from two sources: the invisible God and the Lord Jesus Christ, who was the visible image of the invisible God.

Galatians 1:4 Who gave himself for our sins, that
he might deliver us from this present evil world,
according to the will of God and our Father.

Paul, after his comments in verse 3, further explains the role of Christ in verse 4. He delivered us. It was not according to his own will, but the will of God "and" our Father. The "and" is *kai* and could have been translated "even" in this case. Surely God and the Father cannot be divided.

Ephesians 1:2 Grace be to you, and peace, from
God our Father, and *from* the Lord Jesus Christ.

We have another similar greeting. The translators added the word *from* so we would understand the meaning better, as in the greeting to the Galatians.

Father Knows Best

Ephesians 1:3 Blessed be the God and Father of our Lord Jesus Christ, who hath blessed us with all spiritual blessings in heavenly places in Christ.

Now Paul looks upon God. God's blessings are found in Christ. Note again the use of *kai*. The word translated as "and" clearly means "even" in this case, but either word conveys the meaning, as in the previous verse.

Ephesians 1:17 That the God of our Lord Jesus Christ, the Father of glory, may give unto you the spirit of wisdom and revelation in the knowledge of him.

Again, Paul's view is focused on God the Father, and he then directs the readers to the Lord Jesus Christ. This is similar to Ephesians 1:3.

Ephesians 3:14 For this cause, I bow my knees unto the Father of our Lord Jesus Christ.

This, again, is similar to verses analyzed earlier. Notice that the Father is not mentioned alone, but this is leading the way to Christ, who is the incarnation of God. This is true in every one of the Father/Son combinations in the Pauline epistles.

Questions Oneness Pentecostals Don't Ask

Ephesians 4:6 One God and Father of all, who is above all, and through all, and in you all.

First, we point out that the first *kai* implies "even," as in previous passages. Then, we notice something quite interesting. God the Father is now able to appear *in* you all. If he is able to do that, then God must also be the Holy Spirit!

Ephesians 5:20 Giving thanks always for all things unto God and the Father in the name of our Lord Jesus Christ.

Here again, Paul writes: God, *kai* (even) the Father. We give him thanks in the name of Jesus!

Ephesians 6:23 Peace be to the brethren, and love with faith, from God the Father and the Lord Jesus Christ.

Paul ends his letter with these words. Notice that in the final verse (Grace be with them that love our Lord Jesus Christ in sincerity), he concentrates on the Lord Jesus Christ alone. Paul never compares loving God and loving Christ to loving two separate persons.

Philippians 1:2 Peace be to the brethren, and love with faith, from God the Father and the Lord Jesus Christ.

This greeting, of course, is similar to those we saw in Romans, Corinthians, Galatians, and Ephesians.

> *Philippians 2:11* And that every tongue should confess that Jesus Christ is Lord, to the glory of God the Father.

Many theologians have argued over the Christology in this verse but have missed the most important point. This verse is part of a whole thought (Chapter 2:3–13). The subject of this passage is something we all need: humility. Christ thought it not robbery to be equal to, or the same as, God in his role of *authority*. But he humbled himself as a man, even unto the cross. Because of that, God the Father exalted him. We should all take that as our example. If we humble ourselves, God will exalt us.

> *Philippians 4:20* Now unto God and our Father be glory for ever and ever.

This verse is sandwiched between two others: Philippians 4:19 "But my God shall supply all your need according to his riches in glory by Christ Jesus" and Philippians 4:21 "Salute every saint in Christ Jesus." Both of them center on Christ. But this passage centers on God the Father. Though the personas of God the Father and Christ Jesus are different, Paul is not concerned with teaching about it.

> Colossians 1:2 To the saints and faithful brethren in Christ which are at Colossae: Grace be unto you, and peace, from God our Father and the Lord Jesus Christ.

This verse starts the well known teaching on the deity of Christ in Paul's letter to the Colossians. Paul begins the letter as he did the others. Notice the first use of *kai*: saints are not different from faithful brethren; they are the same people. In this case, the word *kai* links them together. Again, there are multiple ways to translate any word.

The remainder of the verse is similar to the others we have studied.

> *Colossians 1:3* We give thanks to God and the Father of our Lord Jesus Christ, praying always for you.

Once again, the focus on God the Father is combined with the Lord Jesus Christ. The next verse (Col 1:4) speaks particularly of their faith, which he has heard they have "in Christ Jesus."

> *Colossians 1:12* Giving thanks unto the Father, which hath made us meet to be partakers of the inheritance of the saints in light:

It is God who has done this. He has delivered us, as the next passage reads, into the kingdom of the Son. The kingdom of God would not be available without the blood and work of Jesus Christ, the Son.

> *Colossians 2:2–3* That their hearts might be comforted, being knit together in love, and unto all riches of the full assurance of understanding, to the acknowledgement of the mystery of God, and of the Father, and of Christ: In whom are hid all the treasures of wisdom and knowledge."

The key word is "mystery." The incarnation is indeed a great mystery. So is the interplay between the two[77] personas. But we must recognize that flesh and blood cannot receive revelation from heaven; the natural, the carnal mind profits nothing in the things of God.

Notice that wisdom and knowledge are in one person singularly: in Christ. There might be a mystery of God, and of the Father, and of Christ, but it is all in Christ. A few verses later, Paul proclaims that the fullness of the Godhead is in him bodily (Col 2:9).

> *Colossians 3:17* And whatsoever ye do in word or deed, do all in the name of the Lord Jesus, giving thanks to God and the Father by him.

---

[77] Paul does not list three here, but two.

Once again, Paul links together the Lord Jesus and God the Father. This time he mentions Jesus first and then points to God the Father. When we do all things in the name of the Lord Jesus, God is honored.

> *1 Thessalonians 1:1–3* Paul, and Silvanus, and Timotheus, unto the church of the Thessalonians which is in God the Father and in the Lord Jesus Christ: Grace be unto you, and peace, from God our Father, and the Lord Jesus Christ. We give thanks to God always for you all, making mention of you in our prayers; Remembering without ceasing your work of faith, and labour of love, and patience of hope in our Lord Jesus Christ, in the sight of God and our Father.

Three times in three verses Paul mentions God our Father and the Lord Jesus Christ. Again, he is referring to the Creator and to the Redeemer. He makes no effort to go beyond this point and to deal with either separation of persons or the unity of the personas. He is greeting the church and then goes on to give practical instructions.

> *1 Thessalonians 1:9–10* For they themselves shew of us what manner of entering in we had unto you, and how ye turned to God from idols to serve the living and true God; And to wait for his Son from heaven, whom he

raised from the dead, *even* Jesus, which delivered us from the wrath to come.

Paul rejoices that the Thessalonian believers now "serve the true and living God" and will wait for "his Son" from heaven. He has no problem seeing these two personas in different lights. The verses are not teaching about the oneness of God nor the truth of the deity of Christ. The genre is eschatological.[78]

1 Thessalonians 3:11 Now God himself and our Father, and our Lord Jesus Christ, direct[79] our way unto you.

We again notice the word for both instances of "and" is *kai*. Again, there is no distinction between God and our Father. The word "even" would have also been correct. The second *kai*, however, is truly "and," taken in light of the other passages of Paul. But as in the other passages, Paul makes no effort to give further explanation.

---

[78] In other words, he is talking about the very end of things.

[79] Comments on the word "direct" were already addressed previously in chapter 9.

🐘Questions Oneness Pentecostals Don't Ask

1 Thessalonians 3:13 To the end he may stablish your hearts unblameable in holiness before God, even our Father, at the coming of our Lord Jesus Christ with all his saints.

This verse comes, of course, two verses after the last verse we analyzed. God *kai* our Father is simply "even." Paul looks forward to the return of the incarnate flesh of the Son of God. God himself is not coming back; he always has been and always will be. Jesus is coming back.

2 Thessalonians 2:1–2: Paul, and Silvanus, and Timotheus, unto the church of the Thessalonians in God our Father and the Lord Jesus Christ: Grace unto you, and peace, from God our Father and the Lord Jesus Christ.

Paul's greeting is similar to the others we have seen.

2 Thessalonians 2:16 Now our Lord Jesus Christ himself, and God, even our Father, which hath loved us, and hath given us everlasting consolation and good hope through grace,

Again, we have *kai* before "God." In accordance with the rest of Paul's writings, we see "and" as the correct translation. It is, of course, very clear that the second *kai* is "even" our Father.

> *1 Timothy 1:2* Unto Timothy, my own son in the faith: Grace, mercy, and peace, from God our Father and Jesus Christ our Lord.

The greeting to Timothy is the same as the other greetings. There is an addition here, though. The other greetings listed "grace and peace," but now we have "grace, mercy, and peace." As Paul is writing these pastoral letters, he includes mercy from God and from the Lord Jesus Christ. I think every minister needs mercy! We cannot be certain that Paul added this purposefully to make a difference from the other epistles, but it is amusing to note it. There is no need for further comments regarding the rest of this.

> *1 Timothy 2:5* There is one God, and one mediator between God and men, the man Christ Jesus.

This is "the truth" (according to 1 Tim 2:4) that Paul wanted to convey. There is one invisible God of the universe, and there is also a man—Christ Jesus, who gave himself for us. Paul is not dealing with the one-ness of personas, but the two magnificent truths: there forever has been one God, and now there is the sacrifice Jesus made for us.

This does not diminish the truth of the deity of Christ, but this passage focuses on the humanity of Christ.

> *2 Timothy 1:2* To Timothy, my dearly beloved son: Grace, mercy, and peace, from God the Father and Christ Jesus our Lord.

This is similar to Paul's greeting in his first letter to Timothy.

> *Titus 1:4* To Titus, mine own son after the common faith: Grace, mercy, and peace, from God the Father and the Lord Jesus Christ our Saviour.

Paul is greeting another of his sons in the gospel. Titus was over the isle of Crete, Timothy over Ephesus. Once again, Paul brings "grace, mercy, and peace" from two sources: creation and redemption.

> *Titus 2:13* Looking for that blessed hope, and the glorious appearing of the great God and our Saviour Jesus Christ.

The Greek text is notably clearer than the other greetings in showing the one-ness of God, magnifying the great divinity of Jesus Christ. Adam Clarke said that the phrase should read: "Looking for that blessed hope, and the appearing of the glory of the *great God, even our Savior Jesus Christ.*"[80]

Every other version outside of the KJV reads the same way: "the appearing of the glory of our great God and Savior, Jesus Christ." John Chrysostom (the well-known theologian of the fourth century who wrote in Greek) said the same thing, pointing out that the appearing of the great God will actually be Christ, since the Father is invisible.[81] It is refreshing to see Paul call Jesus our "Great God!"

> *Philemon 1:3* Grace to you, and peace, from God our Father and the Lord Jesus Christ.

This greeting is consistent with the others we saw earlier from Paul.

This concludes our brief study of the Pauline epistles. Now we go on to the "general epistles" of James, Peter, John, and Jude.

---

[80] Adam Clarke, *Commentary*: Titus 2:13. Italics mine. Also see his comments on Ephesians 5:5.

[81] Chrysostom, *Fifth Homily of Chrysostom*, "Epistle of Titus." The earliest postapostolic writings of Clement, Ignatius, and others also called Christ "our God."

James 1:17 Every good gift and every perfect gift is from above, and cometh down from the Father of lights, with whom is no variableness, neither shadow of turning.

The focus here is on God the Father. Unlike what we find in Paul's writings, the passage is not linked to Christ.[82]

James 1:27 Pure religion and undefiled before God and the Father is this, to visit the fatherless and widows in their affliction, and to keep himself unspotted from the world.

Once again, we realize the word *kai* could have been translated "even." In this passage, James again refers to God the Father without mentioning Christ. It is unusual, but his letter mentions very little about the gospel. Instead it is a practical book, often called the "Proverbs of the New Testament."

James 3:9 Therewith bless we God, even the Father; and therewith curse we men, which are made after the similitude of God.

---

[82] Of course it is linked theologically, but we are examining each passage individually.

Father Knows Best

This is the third time James mentions God the Father.[83] The *kai* is correctly translated as "even" in this case. Each of these three passages mentions only God and not Christ.

Now we can finally examine the writings of Peter. This is important for a few reasons. First, he was the chief apostle, speaking for the others on the day of Pentecost. He received from Jesus the keys to open the doors to the church (Mt 16:19). Second, he received the revelation of the identity of Christ, and Jesus said this came from God, not man (Mt 16:17). He would have heard the words of Jesus to baptize in the "name of the Father and of the Son and of the Holy Ghost" (Mt 28:19), but he commanded all to be baptized in the name of Jesus (Acts 2, 8, 10). Third, Peter was there when Jesus was transfigured (Mt 17, Mk 8, Lk 9).

> *1 Peter 1:2* Elect according to the foreknowledge of God the Father, through sanctification of the Spirit, unto obedience and sprinkling of the blood of Jesus Christ: Grace unto you, and peace, be multiplied.

---

[83] Most feel like this book was written by James the Less, who was probably the half-brother of Jesus.

This passage is often used to support the doctrine of the Trinity. However, it is important to note the difference between what developed as the *modern* Trinity and Peter's remarks. Did he understand the personas of the Father, the Spirit, and the Son? This verse shows that he did. But there is a big difference between personas and later doctrines of "persons." Peter said nothing in this epistle of an "eternal Son."[84] Nor did he speak of "coequal, coeternal persons"— terms that were developed in the fourth century.

> *1 Peter 1:3* Blessed be the God and Father of our Lord Jesus Christ, which according to his abundant mercy hath begotten us again unto a lively hope by the resurrection of Jesus Christ from the dead.

Peter highlights the view of the Father of the Lord Jesus Christ. Our experience of being begotten comes from God. Yes, we could say that we were begotten by the Spirit, or by Christ, but this passage says we were begotten by God the Father. Although we could fight endless battles trying to identify correctly the persona who begat us, Peter is emphasizing that the original authority of all is God the Father.

---

[84] This term was first used by Clement of Alexandria, AD 150–215. (Chapter 12, *Exhortation to the Heathen*, public domain)

Father Knows Best

1 Peter 1:17 And if ye call on the Father, who without respect of persons judgeth according to every man's work, pass the time of your sojourning here in fear.

Once again, Peter brings attention to the Father. In particular, knowing that there is a God who sees all, hears all, and knows all rightfully causes us to live with godly fear and holiness.

2 Peter 1:17 For he received from God the Father honour and glory, when there came such a voice to him from the excellent glory, This is my beloved Son, in whom I am well pleased.

Peter's intention is to validate Christ as the Son of God. As we mentioned, Peter himself was there (Mt. 17) and had personally witnessed this event. He heard the voice and saw the supernatural events of that day. This gave him a surety that Jesus was more than a man; he was the Son of God. He is not teaching the one-ness of personas in this case. Some will ask, how could God speak, yet Christ was there? The answer is that while Jesus was here, God could still be above all things and speak from heaven!

Questions Oneness Pentecostals Don't Ask

The Letters of John

Now we can begin investigating the letters of John the beloved. If any person could say that he saw Jesus in his glory, it was John. In his fearful vision at Patmos, he lay at his feet as if dead. Jesus put his hand upon him and said, "I am the Alpha and Omega, the beginning and the ending, the first and the last. I am the Almighty. I was dead, and now I am alive forevermore. I have the keys of hell and of death" (Rev. 1:8, 11, 17–18). John had heard Thomas call Jesus "My Lord and My God" (John 20:28). Now he confirms to all of us that this man Jesus is the "KING OF KINGS AND LORDS OF LORDS!" (Rev. 19:16; see also Rev. 17:14).[85]

In today's world, all Christians take it for granted that God is the Father of all, and Christ is the Son of God. But then, the issues must be wrestled out: Is Christ another Person? Or is he the same as God? Our questions are based on this: we already assume that both God and Christ are in heaven and are God. But John lived in a different time than we do.

First, he believed in God. God the Father had always been God, and he will never change. John knew that. Second, John knew the man Jesus. He had leaned against his bosom and had actually handled the Word of life. Then Jesus, later in his resurrected state, tells him "I am the first and the last," (Rev 1:11) just as God had said of himself (Isa 44:6).

---

[85] Caps as with KJV.

It is this addition to deity that mystifies all of us. Can anyone say, in all honesty, that they firmly grasp it all? The revelation of Christ, and the Almighty God in him for us, is almost easy in comparison. But when God, who is invisible, adds humanity to the "package," it boggles our mind. Yet God was able to find a way, through the incarnation, to save us.

Let's revisit our question. Do we say that Jesus was the Son of God, or Jesus was God? Once again, it is not either-or but both-and. Both proclamations have scriptures for support. The awesome mystery of this is that the Father of creation was manifested in life as the Son. Yet he was still God.

Let's go back to John in his time. He loves God, and he loves Jesus. So we have an additional persona—actually the element of humanity that was not there before the incarnation. To understand this, we need to look at John's gospel.

His writing begins by subtly alluding to the creation of the world. The same word that John used for "beginning," *arche*, was used in Genesis 1:1 in the Septuagint, the Greek version of the Old Testament. He connected the beginning of all creation with the beginning of God's salvation by starting his gospel with "In the beginning."

Now, let's look at another important word. In his gospel, John writes: "In the beginning was the *Word*." The Greek was *logos*. It meant the thought, the light, the life of God. But what or who was the *logos*? Was it God the Father, who created the world and all that it contains? Or was it the man Jesus that walked on the streets of Capernaum? I submit it was both. The *logos* linked these two together: God the Father and Christ Jesus. Watch the meaning of the word *logos* change from God the Father to Jesus Christ in the first chapter of his gospel.

John starts his gospel indicating that the *logos*, though with God, is truly God. My word is part of me, but it is me. It is the same with God. The Word and God are equals. The Greek of John 1:1 puts it like this: In the beginning was the Word, and the Word was with God, and God was the Word. Then, in John 1:2–9, the light shines in the darkness, and darkness cannot stop the light. Obviously, we are talking about God. No one can stop him.

But in John 1:10–14, John further explains the *logos*: "He was in the world, and the world was made by him, and the world knew him not." But some did receive him and became the sons of God! Of whom is he speaking? God made the world; he spoke it into existence (Gen 1, Psalm 33:6). But some received him? We are made to wonder: Is John possibly also talking about this man Jesus?

John the Baptist came to bear witness of the light. But now the light is a man! John makes this plain for us when he declares that "the Word was made flesh and dwelt among us" (John 1:14)!

The *logos* took on human nature! Did the "Eternal" Son of God take on this nature? No, this was God himself. John the Baptist declared, "He that comes after me ... was before me"! (John 1:15, 1:27)

How should John speak of both God the Father and Christ? From the beginning of this epistle to the exceptionally brilliant last verse, he moves from the "practical" two-ness view of the Father *and* the Son to the "revelational" one-ness view of the Father *in* the Son.[86] There is no other way for John to express this but in these following letters.

> *1 John 1:1–3* That which was from the beginning, which we have heard, which we have seen with our eyes, which we have looked upon, and our hands have handled, of the Word of life (For the life was manifested, and we have seen it, and bear witness, and shew unto you that eternal life, which was with the Father, and was manifested unto us); That which we have seen and heard declare we unto you, that ye also may have fellowship with us: and truly our fellowship is with the Father, and with his Son Jesus Christ.

Notice the treatment of the "life" that manifested. Life was with God and is now manifested to us. This very eternal life that is manifested is actually in the man from Galilee! John treats the word "life" in these verses much as he did in the part of his gospel dealing with both "life" and "light." Life and fellowship are with the Father *and* with the Son!

---

[86] Please refer to chapter 3, "Let Me Count the Ways." We said there are three ways to count the personas of God: the obvious (three-ness), the practical (two-ness), and the revelational (one-ness).

John testifies about his own experience (and that of others): our eyes have seen and our hands have actually handled the Word. This Word came from heaven. It was with God, yet it was God all by itself. We do not just have fellowship with God, but with the man that once walked the shores of time.

1 John 2:1 My little children, these things write I unto you, that ye sin not. And if any man sin, we have an advocate with the Father, Jesus Christ the righteous:

This is where the distinctions between the personas can make sense. We are judged by God, but Jesus Christ stands in the gap as our lawyer. We earlier alluded to David Bernard's remarks about the change of clothes. The judge put on the lawyer's clothing. That is a beautiful way to put this. Yet we still need to understand the roles of the personas. God, in the role of judge, calls us to repentance. Jesus, in the role of our Redeemer on the cross, provides pardon for our sins.[87]

---

[87] A little nugget: Jesus is our "advocate." Some versions use "lawyer." The Greek word is *parakletos*. We also find this word, *parakletos*, translated to the word "Comforter" in John 14:16, 14:26, 16:26, and 16:7. So is the Comforter, which is Holy Spirit, another, different persona than the Son? Yes, in its purest theology. Yet we find John refers to the *parakletos* as both the "third person" in his gospel and the "second person" in his epistle.

Father Knows Best

1 John 2:13, 15–16 I write unto you, fathers, because ye have known him that is from the beginning. I write unto you, young men, because ye have overcome the wicked one. I write unto you, little children, because ye have known the Father. Love not the world, neither the things that are in the world. If any man love the world, the love of the Father is not in him. For all that is in the world, the lust of the flesh, and the lust of the eyes, and the pride of life, is not of the Father, but is of the world.

John is not afraid to note the Father as God. He makes no mention of Christ in this passage. The question might be asked. Why did John mention fathers and their sons? I submit this possibility: John implies that the relation that fathers have with their children, and also children have with their fathers, may help us understand the Father in heaven.

1 John 2:22–25 Who is a liar but he that denieth that Jesus is the Christ? He is antichrist, that denieth the Father and the Son. Whosoever denieth the Son, the same hath not the Father: [but] he that acknowledgeth the Son hath the Father also.[88] Let that therefore abide in you, which ye

---

[88] This phrase is in italics in KJV, indicating an addition. But there are good arguments that these words were in the original Greek. See Adam Clarke's commentary on 1 John 2:23.

have heard from the beginning. If that which ye
have heard from the beginning shall remain in
you, ye also shall continue in the Son, and in the
Father. And this is the promise that he hath promised us, even eternal life.

If someone denies Christ, he is a liar. He denies not only God but the incarnation. If he acknowledges the incarnation, he has God.

As the "New Issue" began exploding in the 1910s, some preachers used 1 John 2:22 to say that Oneness Pentecostals were part of the spirit of the Antichrist. The Oneness response was to note verse 23. If the Son is acknowledged, then so is the Father! If we continue in the Son, we are continuing in the Father. We shall continue in the Son and—*kai*—in the Father. If the *kai* was meant in this case to separate the Son from the Father, making them two distinct persons, we would have a problem with the last verse: "*He* hath (not *they* have) promised us even eternal life"!

1 John 3:1 Behold, what manner of love the Father
hath bestowed upon us, that we should be called
the sons of God: therefore the world knoweth us
not, because it knew him not.

As before, John refers to God as the Father. He is the one that has given us love. Although we could consider the other personas, it surely is not wrong for John to put the emphasis as he did in this passage.

> *1 John 4:14* And we have seen and do testify that the Father sent the Son to be the Saviour of the world.

God the Father by himself could not save us. He wanted to save us, but he had to find a "legal" way to do this. He sent this remedy for sin. This should not keep us from acknowledging that God was in Christ, but here we speak of the personas separately.

> *1 John 5:7* For there are three that bear record in heaven, the Father, the Word, and the Holy Ghost: and these three are one.

This passage is worth noting. Three what? It does not say. So we have wrestled through the centuries to find words: persons, offices, manifestations, roles, modes, modes of being, and personas. But these three are one. However, let us take a closer look. This passage does not say the Father, the Son, and the Holy Ghost are one. Instead, the Father, the *Word*, and the Holy Ghost are one.[89] The Son is something

---

[89] The Spirit, the blood, and the water may *agree* in one, but the Father, Word, and Spirit *are* one.

the Father was not before the incarnation. But the Word—the Logos—always was. Many think this passage was added to the text later. Here is an interesting point to note. If that did happen, we know it had to be before the Trinitarian terminology developed. Otherwise, it would been the "Father, the *Son*, and Holy Ghost" are one.

> *1 John 5:20* We are in him that is true, even in his Son Jesus Christ. This is the true God, and eternal life.

This is a wonderful way for John to end his first epistle! Eternal life of God is found in his Son Jesus. He that has the Son has life (1 John 5:12)! Now, let's move over to the revelational side of the elephant: the Son is the true God![90]

> *2 John 1:3* Grace be with you, mercy, and peace, from God the Father, and from the Lord Jesus Christ, the Son of the Father, in truth and love.

Like Paul, John says there are two founts: one comes from God as the Creator and the other from the Redeemer on the cross. The *kai* links the founts, but not the personas.

---

[90] The next verse reads, "Keep yourself from idols." John was not referring to the theory of a coequal Trinity, since the doctrine had not yet been developed. The remark probably refers to the battle against Docetism and Gnosticism.

This is clear, since John gives a definition of the Lord Jesus Christ, the "Son of the Father."

> *2 John 1:9* Whosoever transgresseth, and abideth not in the doctrine of Christ, hath not God. He that abideth in the doctrine of Christ, he hath both the Father and the Son.

If we do not abide in Christ, we do not have God. If we abide in Christ, the roles of both God the Creator and the Son as Redeemer are working in us. The invisible God and the visible image of the invisible God are with us. We have both the Father and the Son.

> *Jude 1:2* Jude, the servant of Jesus Christ, and brother of James, to them that are sanctified by God the Father, and preserved in Jesus Christ, and called:

This greeting is similar to the others, especially those of Paul. It would be a stretch to *confine* the roles of the Father to sanctification and of Christ to preservation. But Jude is recognizing two: the invisible God, the Father, and the visible image of the invisible God, Jesus Christ.

Conclusion

Admittedly, this has been a very difficult study. I would much rather meditate on the virtues of Christ, attach my life to the cross, and wait on God in the face of Jesus Christ.[91]

We do rejoice in the revelation that Jesus Christ is our God. In both Titus 2:13 and 1 John 2:20, the one-ness brings us clarity about the deity of Christ. But it has only been fair and honest to look at the two-ness passages as well. After all, these passages raise questions that Oneness Pentecostals don't ask.

Most of the two-ness passages in the epistles, particularly with Paul, have the purpose of introduction but not teaching. Peter's two-ness passage (2 Peter 1:17) is the closest we have to what some believe to be a separation of persons. But the point of this text is to exalt Jesus as the Son of God (not just a man), as we have seen. John's passages start with two-ness and then lead us into the deity of Christ. God is in Christ, and we can find God there—both the Father and the Son.

When we consider the three-ness passages in the epistles, we only have two. Paul's benediction (2 Cor 13:14) does not stress the same functions as we would expect in pure Trinitarian teaching. Peter does mention the three (1 Peter 1:2) in their functions, but as we have seen, he does not go any further.

---

[91] 2 Corinthians 4:6 "For God, who commanded the light to shine out of darkness, hath shined in our hearts, to give the light of the knowledge of the glory of God in the face of Jesus Christ."

SUMMARY AND REFLECTIONS

At some point we need to leave the mystery of the Godhead, like other things unknown, in the hands of God. I do realize the analogy of the elephant could be considered trite and not worthy of who God is.

We selected the word "personas" in this study. Is there really a difference between personas and persons? Is not "God in three personas" the same thing as "God in three persons"? I do understand this question. I *can* see God as the Father, as the Son, as the Spirit. But there are two answers. First, there is a major difference between a persona (a mask, a way that God shows up) and a person (an individual with separate thinking abilities and decisions). Second, a preexistent second person did not come down from heaven. It was God who was manifested as the son of man. It was God who was in Christ, paying our debt of sin.

I stated in the Preface that this book was written for two sets of readers. If you have not seen the mighty God in Christ and the Apostolic message, this book has been partly written for you. The apostles were asked what to do on the first day of the church, the day of Pentecost. Peter very clearly replied:

> Repent, and be baptized every one of you in the name of Jesus Christ for the remission of sins, and ye shall receive the gift of the Holy Ghost. For the promise is unto you, and to your children and to all that are afar off (Acts 2:38–39).

I think it is plain that this is the pattern that was followed throughout the first church in Acts. I believe Oneness Pentecostalism does "get it" on two major issues: soteriology—how to be saved (Acts 2:38), and the deity of Christ. Regarding the first issue, certainly the understanding of Oneness Pentecostals is biblical. It surely does more for the soul than just repeating a prayer. On the second issue, let me explain.

The revelation of Christ does something wonderful to our understanding of God. It is almost like the change from black-and-white movies. They were nice, but when movies were produced in living color, the images were as

Summary and Reflections

real as life. God became visible to us in living color through Jesus Christ. The mysterious God becomes life to us.

This indeed is a big God we believe in. I wish we could say we know everything, but we do not. We are still learning, still reaching, still attempting to be "Apostolic" as the first church was. I'm glad we have the water–Spirit doctrine of Acts. In a doctrinal sense, we are indeed Apostolic when we follow the first Church in this matter. But the first church had much more than this.

We have taken over a century[92] to make sure we have Acts 2 down. But what about Acts 3 to 28? It was the miracle of healing in Acts 3 that really sparked revival (and persecution) in Jerusalem. We need to be apostolic by "diverse miracles and gifts of the Holy Ghost" (Hebrews 2:4) so we may "fully preach the gospel" (Romans 15:19). I don't think it was just the sign by itself. It was the power that was in Peter's heart. As an outgrowth of his experience with God, he reached out his hand to the needy. Paraphrasing Peter, he looked at the lame man, giving him hope: "I don't have money, but I do have something from heaven! Let me help you." We need that sort of experience again in our people. If we need to reach out for more, then we should also help others to do the same.

---

[92] "Over a century" is referring to the time since the Apostolic Faith Worldwide Camp Meeting at Arroyo Seco in 1913. In 1919 the Pentecostal Assemblies of the World, the first major Oneness group, was incorporated. Out of this came two major Oneness groups, both beginning in 1924.

Questions Oneness Pentecostals Don't Ask

Frank Ewart, many years after spearheading the Oneness movement, wrote:

> Every unit of Christianity has the apparent characteristic of turning the life stream of Calvary into a sectarian channel. They announce, by the introduction of particular and distinctive laws and rules regarding fellowship, their belief that life and power depend upon a correct system of doctrine.... Do not misunderstand me. We cannot do without doctrine. But no doctrinal truth, however ennobling, can save a human soul from death. They must be saved by a Person, only a Person, and by One Person.[93]

Ewart was not saying that we should not have doctrine. Neither am I. The early Church continued in it (Acts 2:42). Those who labor therein are to be esteemed highly (1 Timothy 5:17). But just give me a fresh glimpse of Jesus. From there, everything else follows.

I am not so arrogant to think that we understand it all. God has not called me to be judge and jury. Yet I refuse to give up the obviously scriptural revelations of God. I cannot be so tolerant that I fail to call an error what it is. With all due respect to my fellow admirers of this elephant, the

---

[93] Frank Ewart, *The Name and the Book*, (Hazelwood, MO: Word Aflame Press, 1986) 105–6.

Summary and Reflections

trend toward tritheism abounds in the creeds, especially the later ones. Yes, I realize we are accused of the opposite error, the so-called simplicity[94] of modalism. I have attempted to respond to this in chapter 4, "Don't Confound the Persons." Yet allow me to say that this book has been an honest attempt to acknowledge any possible warts on both of our faces.

In a way, we are all hanging around the same elephant. In truth, we are all so blind. So what do we do? Well, if we are curious enough, if we get close enough, we might just feel his heartbeat. And if we could actually hear his heart, would it almost talk? What would it say unto us? It would be nothing less than Jesus. The most magnificent miracle that ever took place is the incarnation of God in the man Jesus Christ. He lived, he loved, and he gave. He died upon a cruel cross to take our place. After rising from the dead, he is alive forevermore. After all is said and done, he will forever be the King of kings and Lord of lords. That is the very heart of this creature.

At least that is how *I* see the elephant.

---

[94] I am referring to the remarks of Tertullian in *Against Praxeas*: "The simple, indeed,—I will not call them unwise and unlearned, who always constitute the majority of believers, are startled at the dispensation (of the Three in One), on the ground that their very rule of faith withdraws them from the world's plurality of gods to the one only true God. ...They are constantly throwing out against us that we are preachers of two gods and three gods, while they take to themselves preeminently the credit of being worshippers of the One God; just as if the Unity itself with irrational deductions did not produce heresy."

Questions Oneness Pentecostals Don't Ask

Addendum I:

On the Errors of the Trinity[95]

Much of this book has pointed to errors in the doctrine of the Trinity, especially in later stages of its development. Therefore, it might be wise to make just a few more comments on its history and why I believe there were errors.

First, there were no evil intentions to imitate the Egyptian gods. That was a different time frame and land than the Greek world between AD 100 and AD 500.

However, there *was* an attempt to reconcile Greek philosophy with the Christian religion. The merging of the two worlds would say that God could not possibly be the one that would be incarnated. He was too aloof from his created beings to do that. So, it had to be just a part of God that would come to earth—the *logos*.

The efforts of the councils, according to the final major creed, the Athanasian Creed, were intended to not confound the persons and to not divide the substance. This remark indicates that both modalism and tritheism were to

---

[95] *On the Errors of the Trinity* is the name Michael Servetus' book, published in 1531. He was burned at the stake for his beliefs on October 27, 1553.

be avoided. The tri-unity of God, the Trinity, was an effort to meet in the middle. Let's examine the brief history of this effort through the creed to see if the efforts were successful.

The first major council (Nicaea, AD 325) called Jesus "very [true] God of very [true] God." The creed ended with an "anathema." That rebuke was not quite against tritheism *per se* but the extreme dualism of Arianism. Very little was said about the Holy Spirit.

But the next councils changed things. When the Nicene Creed was revised at Constantinople (AD 381), it said quite a bit about the Holy Spirit. He was to be worshiped "with the Father and with the Son." This creed also touched on the theory of eternal generation—the idea that Christ was born "before all ages." This version of the Nicene Creed is the one currently used.

The next creed, written at the council of Chalcedon (AD 451), reiterated the doctrine of eternal generation. Christ was born of the Father before all ages *and* was also born in Bethlehem.

The Athanasian Creed of the late fifth or early sixth century declared the "Father uncreated, the Son uncreated, and the Spirit uncreated." These "three persons are coeternal and coequal." Also, "none is greater or less than another." Although modalism was avoided, tritheism was not.[96]

---

[96] Admittedly the Athanasian Creed does say there are not three gods, but one God. See the Creed itself in the next addendum: point # 16. However, points #8, 10, and 25 were also considered for my statement.

On the Errors of the Trinity

There are two errors in the doctrine of the Trinity as it developed. The first one is the preexistence of the Son. How could the Son have existed in all eternity, and yet God said no one was with him in the Old Testament?

The second is its doctrine of the Holy Spirit. It (or he) was exalted as a "person" having the features of its own being, much as the doctrine had spoken of the Father and the Son.

Consider this: the God of the ages that hated sin took on the form of man to take mankind's place on the cross. He had made the heavens, the earth, the sea and the dry land. There was no other god with him. This God was actually in Jesus Christ, reconciling the world unto himself. He became the second Adam. This substitution made for us must be understood by faith, not just by the intellect.

My conclusion is that the doctrine of the Trinity developed because of attempts to explain intellectually something that is revealed only by the Spirit.

Addendum II:

The Major Creeds of the Postapostolic Church

THE APOSTLE'S CREED[97]

1. I believe in God the Father Almighty, Maker of heaven and earth:
2. And in Jesus Christ, his only Son, our Lord:
3. Who was conceived by the Holy Ghost, born of the Virgin Mary:
4. Suffered under Pontius Pilate; was crucified, dead, and buried: He descended into hell:
5. The third day he rose again from the dead:
6. He ascended into heaven, and sitteth at the right hand of God the Father Almighty:
7. From thence he shall come to judge the quick [living] and the dead:
8. I believe in the Holy Ghost:
9. I believe in the Holy Catholic Church: the communion of saints:

---

[97] Notice twelve points. A legendary thought was that each Apostle wrote a different statement.

10. The forgiveness of sins:
11. The resurrection of the body:
12. And the life everlasting. Amen.

THE NICENE CREEDS
Original (325) and Revised (381) Versions Compared[98]

The Nicene Creed of 325.	The Revised Nicene Creed of 381.
We believe in one God, the Father Almighty, Maker of all things visible and invisible.	We believe in one God, the Father Almighty, Maker of heaven and earth, and of all things visible and invisible.
And in one Lord Jesus Christ, the Son of God, begotten of the Father, the only-begotten; that is, of the essence of the Father, God of God, Light of Light, very [true] God of very [true] God, begotten, not made, being of one substance with the Father; by whom all things were made both in heaven and on earth; who for us men, and for our salvation,	And in one Lord Jesus Christ, the only-begotten Son of God, begotten of the Father before all worlds, Light of Light, very [true] God of very [true] God, begotten, not made, being of one substance with the Father; by whom all things were made; who for us men, and for our salvation, came down from heaven, and was incarnate by the Holy

---

[98] Although the creeds are in public domain, the comparison may be found in Phillip Scaff, *The Creeds of Christendom, with a History and Critical Notes* (New York: Harper & Brothers, 1877), 28–29.

The Major Creeds of the Postapostolic Church

came down and was incarnate and was made man; he suffered, and the third day he rose again, ascended into heaven; from thence he shall come to judge the quick [living] and the dead.	Ghost of the Virgin Mary, and was made man; he was crucified for us under Pontius Pilate, and suffered, and was buried, and the third day he rose again, according to the Scriptures, and ascended into heaven, and sits on the right hand of the Father; from thence he shall come again, with glory, to judge the quick [living] and the dead; whose kingdom shall have no end.
And in the Holy Ghost.	And in the Holy Ghost, the Lord and Giver of life, who proceeds from the Father, who with the Father and the Son together is worshiped and glorified, who spoke by the prophets. In one holy catholic and apostolic Church, we acknowledge one baptism for the remission of sins; we look for the resurrection of the dead, and the life of the world to come. Amen.
But those who say: 'There was a time when he was not;' and 'He was not before he was made;' and 'He was made out of nothing,' or 'He is of another substance' or	

'essence,' or 'The Son of God is created,' or 'changeable,' or 'alterable'—they are condemned by the holy catholic and apostolic Church.	

THE DEFINITION OF CHALCEDON

We all with once voice teach that it is to be confessed that our Lord Jesus Christ is one and the same God, perfect in divinity, and perfect in humanity, true God and true man, with a rational soul and a body, of one substance with the Father in his divinity, in every way like us, with the only exception of sin, begotten of the Father before all ages in his divinity, and also begotten in the latter days, in his humanity of Mary the virgin bearer of God.

THE ATHANASIAN CREED[99]

1. Whosoever will be saved, before all things it is necessary that he hold the catholic faith;
2. Which faith except everyone do keep whole and undefiled, without doubt he shall perish everlastingly.
3. And the catholic faith is this: That we worship one God in Trinity, and Trinity in Unity;

---

[99] The numbered points will aid the reader in the last footnote of Addendum I.

4. Neither confounding the persons nor dividing the substance.
5. For there is one person of the Father, another of the Son, and another of the Holy Spirit.
6. But the Godhead of the Father, of the Son, and of the Holy Spirit is all one, the glory equal, the majesty coeternal.
7. Such as the Father is, such is the Son, and such is the Holy Spirit.
8. The Father uncreated, the Son uncreated, and the Holy Spirit uncreated.
9. The Father incomprehensible, the Son incomprehensible, and the Holy Spirit incomprehensible.
10. The Father eternal, the Son eternal, and the Holy Spirit eternal.
11. And yet they are not three eternals but one eternal.
12. As also there are not three uncreated nor three incomprehensible, but one uncreated and one incomprehensible.
13. So likewise the Father is almighty, the Son almighty, and the Holy Spirit almighty.
14. And yet they are not three almighties, but one almighty.
15. So the Father is God, the Son is God, and the Holy Spirit is God;
16. And yet they are not three Gods, but one God.
17. So likewise the Father is Lord, the Son Lord, and the Holy Spirit Lord;
18. And yet they are not three Lords but one Lord.
19. For like as we are compelled by the Christian verity to acknowledge every Person by himself to be God and Lord;

20. So are we forbidden by the catholic religion to say; There are three Gods or three Lords.
21. The Father is made of none, neither created nor begotten.
22. The Son is of the Father alone; not made nor created, but begotten.
23. The Holy Spirit is of the Father and of the Son; neither made, nor created, nor begotten, but proceeding.
24. So there is one Father, not three Fathers; one Son, not three Sons; one Holy Spirit, not three Holy Spirits.
25. And in this Trinity none is afore or after another; none is greater or less than another.
26. But the whole three persons are coeternal, and coequal.
27. So that in all things, as aforesaid, the Unity in Trinity and the Trinity in Unity is to be worshipped.
28. He therefore that will be saved must thus think of the Trinity.
29. Furthermore it is necessary to everlasting salvation that he also believe rightly the incarnation of our Lord Jesus Christ.
30. For the right faith is that we believe and confess that our Lord Jesus Christ, the Son of God, is God and man.
31. God of the substance of the Father, begotten before the worlds; and man of substance of His mother, born in the world.
32. Perfect God and perfect man, of a reasonable soul and human flesh subsisting.
33. Equal to the Father as touching His Godhead, and inferior to the Father as touching His manhood.

34. Who, although He is God and man, yet He is not two, but one Christ.
35. One, not by conversion of the Godhead into flesh, but by taking of that manhood into God.
36. One altogether, not by confusion of substance, but by unity of person.
37. For as the reasonable soul and flesh is one man, so God and man is one Christ;
38. Who suffered for our salvation, descended into hell, rose again the third day from the dead;
39. He ascended into heaven, He sits on the right hand of the Father, God, Almighty;
40. From thence He shall come to judge the quick and the dead.
41. At whose coming all men shall rise again with their bodies;
42. and shall give account of their own works.
43. And they that have done good shall go into life everlasting and they that have done evil into everlasting fire.
44. This is the catholic faith, which except a man believe faithfully he cannot be saved.

Other Books by the Author

The Development of the Trinity:
The Evolution of a New Doctrine

The Trinity was a new doctrine that developed. This book is replete with nearly 300 footnotes, a section on the history of non-biblical words such as "God the Son," a great summary, and a comprehensive annotated bibliography. The author quotes historians and primary material for the proofs. He charts the step-by-step development of what became the Trinity in three general stages: Father-Son questions, the Holy Spirit added as a person, and three persons in communion. This study details how Christ became, in theology, a pre-existent second "person" in the godhead. The paperback may be obtained at pentecostalpublishing.com; the e-book at pentecostalpublishing.com, amazon.com, or barnesandnoble.com.

This Spanish version of *The Development of the Trinity; The Evolution of a New Doctrine* in paperback may be obtained at Pentecostalpublishing.com. The e-book may be obtained at pentecostalpublishing.com, amazon.com, or barnesandnoble.com.

Other Books by the Author

Jesus' Matters: A Simple Version of The Development of the Trinity

The previous book (*The Development of the Trinity: The Evolution of a New Doctrine*) traces in step-by-step detail the history of the theology of the Trinity, influenced by human logic, from about A.D. 100 to A.D. 500. This book, however, is made for young people and is comparatively simple. It begins with the author's testimony, proceeds to Apostolic teaching, and finally takes on the task of simplifying the historical study of the Trinity from Justin Martyr to St. Augustine. After this, the subject of church history takes the reader from the Reformation era to the present. Then controversial issues are raised: What are the uses of John 3:5? Were Matthew 28:19's words added? The final chapter reflects on the issues of Oneness Pentecostalism and its relationship to the rest of the church world. The paperback may be obtained at pentecostalpublishing.com; the e-book at amazon.com or barnesandnoble.com. (Cover image may be different.)

This Spanish version of *Jesus' Matters* in paperback may be obtained from pentecostalpublishing.com or amazon.com. The title, translated to English, is "The Development of the Trinity—The Simple Version." The e-book may be obtained from amazon.com or barnesandnoble.com. (Cover image may be different.)

Made in the USA
Columbia, SC
21 April 2023